"ENGROSSING, REAL-LIFE EXPLORATION INTO A LITTLE SEEN WORLD."
—*Manchester Union Leader*

"A FUNNY, CANDID AND ENGROSSING CHRONICLE. Haas takes his readers on a roller-coaster ride through his rigorous and demanding year-long training period to become a psychotherapist."
—*Rocky Mountain News*

"Thoughtful, honest . . . provocative."
—*Booklist*

"Offers poignant glimpses of life inside a psychiatric institution."
—*Boston Herald*

SCOTT HAAS, Ph.D., graduated from Hampshire College, attended the University of Detroit, and completed his internship in a Harvard-affiliated Massachusetts hospital. He is currently a consultant to the commonwealth of Massachusetts on the issue of homelessness, and Lecturer in Psychology at Harvard Medical School's Cambridge City Hospital. He lives in Cambridge with his wife and their children. He has recently completed a novel.

SCOTT HAAS, PH.D.

HEARING VOICES

REFLECTIONS OF
A PSYCHOLOGY
INTERN

A PLUME BOOK

PLUME
Published by the Penguin Group
Penguin Books USA Inc., 375 Hudson Street, New York, New York 10014, U.S.A.
Penguin Books Ltd, 27 Wrights Lane, London W8 5TZ, England
Penguin Books Australia Ltd, Ringwood, Victoria, Australia
Penguin Books Canada Ltd, 10 Alcorn Avenue, Toronto, Ontario, Canada M4V 3B2
Penguin Books (N.Z.) Ltd, 182-190 Wairau Road, Auckland 10, New Zealand

Penguin Books Ltd, Registered Offices: Harmondsworth, Middlesex, England

Published by Plume, an imprint of New American Library,
a division of Penguin Books USA Inc.
Previously published in a Dutton edition.

First Plume Printing, December, 1991
10 9 8 7 6 5 4 3 2 1

 REGISTERED TRADEMARK—MARCA REGISTRADA

LIBRARY OF CONGRESS CATALOGING-IN-PUBLICATION DATA
Haas, Scott.
    Hearing voices: reflections of a psychology intern / Scott Haas.
      p.   cm.
    Originally published: New York : Dutton, c1990.
    ISBN 0-452-26705-6
    1. Haas, Scott.   2. Interns (Clinical psychology)—Massachusetts—
Cambridge—Biography.   3. Psychotherapy—Study and teaching—
Massachusetts—Cambridge.   4. Commonwealth Mental Health Institute
(Cambridge, Mass.)   I. Title.
    [DNLM: 1. Internship and Residency.   2. Massachusetts.
3. Psychology, Clinical—personal narratives.   4. Psychotherapy—
education—Massachusetts.   WZ 100 H353 1990a]
RC339.52.H3A3   1990b
616.89′14′07155—dc20
DGPO/DLC
for Library of Congress   91-31998
                                                                  CIP

Printed in the United States of America

To my mother and father

ACKNOWLEDGMENTS

Most of all, I thank my wife Laura and my daughter Madeline, whose love makes imaginative work possible.

I am also grateful to the patients I knew during my internship, whose faith in the value of their lives, and whose trust in me, enabled me to listen and learn from them.

My teachers and supervisors remain profoundly important: Mrs. Bartle, Alexander MacDougall, Jacques LeGrand, Robert Marquez, Jon Chodosh, Marie Banerjee, Bernie Green, Marv Hyman, James Keillor, Nick Avery, Bill Beuscher, Margaret Brenman-Gibson, Robert Jay Lifton, John Mack, Mel Barton, and Elizabeth Gourdin.

My fellow psychology interns and psychiatry residents, especially those on day hospital one, helped me immensely during the internship year.

Alexia Dorszynski, my editor, has been a wonderful guide to the possibilities, both surprising and inevitable, inherent in language.

I am also thrilled to be able to thank Malaga Baldi, more than a friend, also an agent.

CONTENTS

He for his part, remembering his arts,
Transformed himself into miraculous shapes
Of every kind—a fire, a fearsome beast.
A flowing stream; but when no trickery
Won him escape, defeated he resumed
His human form, and thus at length began:
"Who then has told you, most presumptuous youth,
To invade my home? What do you want of me?"

—VIRGIL, *The Georgics*

INTRODUCTION

Along with other students in Ph.D. (clinical psychology) and Psy.D. (professional psychology) programs across the country, I applied to internship sites when I had satisfied the requirements of my graduate school. An internship in clinical psychology usually begins after course work (which typically takes three years) and a testing practicum (lasting one year, for about twenty hours per week) are completed, and an M.A. examination and thesis are passed.

I'd had limited experience working with the mentally ill before starting the internship. While an undergraduate at Hampshire College, I worked for six months at the Northampton Veterans Administration hospital as a psychotherapist-trainee for two people who had been diagnosed long before as chronic, paranoid schizophrenics. They had each been institutionalized for at least twenty-five years when I met them. Twice weekly we chatted, mostly about what they remembered of their lives before they became ill. I had no formal supervision, but was given a lot to do because the chief psychologist on the unit said, "You can't really screw up with people as sick as they are, and you'll learn a lot from them." One man made a lasting impression. He was the first mentally ill person I got to know well.

He still had a small reserve of enthusiasm for life, undiluted by his long confinement and illness. Often he was clear and funny. His expressions were highly original, too, as if they had been chiseled into stone. For example, when asked to describe his mother, he declared, "She was a phlegmatic woman." He could not explain her to me any better, and it remains unclear what he meant precisely, or why he spoke with such bland conviction.

I liked him for being definite. It made the remark unforgettable; I have never heard anyone else's mother described this way. Perhaps the uniqueness of the description enabled him to preserve his memory of her, and to keep her separate from everyone else.

He remembered the strangest things about having been a child and young adult. There was the time he tore his pants on barbed wire suspended over a wooden fence, while running from a farmer who chased him and a few other boys down off a cherry tree. He loved the first time he was on his own, in Akron, Ohio, frying up his favorite meal of liver and onions every Friday night in the room that he rented by the week.

I had never met anyone before whose memory was so disparate. It was as if he went from one place to another, never taking along anything substantial. He lived from disconnected images, with idiosyncratic language, and not in relationships.

When he spoke psychotically, which was most of the time, it was to say, in hushed, confidential tones, that he was an hermaphrodite and the FBI was spying on him because of that condition. He imagined seeing them drive by in their black cars, and he hid in his room to avoid them.

I tried hard to talk him out of his delusions. I presented lots of facts to contradict him. Finally, exasperated, he turned to me and said, "You'd probably go crazy, too, if you'd been through what I been through."

His psychosis was the best he could do to stay human.

Without it, his suffering made no sense. Ironically, madness made him more of a person.

During graduate school, I also worked as a therapist at the university's out-patient clinic. I saw a few adults and children. I was provided with weekly supervision by a clinical psychologist. Each case was presented for discussion to a clinician at a case conference. I also gained experience during a twenty-hour per week testing practicum. Using psychological tests, I evaluated in-patients at the Detroit Psychiatric Institute, interpreting results from a psychoanalytic perspective.

Other than these experiences, most of my knowledge about clinical work with the mentally ill came from texts by Freud, Jung, Rank, Reich, Reik, Sullivan, Erikson, Winnicott, Kohut, Kernberg, and others.

A psychology internship is, roughly, the final stage in the formal training process toward becoming a clinical psychologist. Although other learning experiences follow, few are quite so rigorous and demanding. As a result, the internship is central to one's development. It is during the internship that one begins to assume the responsibility of being the primary clinician: to organize fully the treatment plan for someone who is judged mentally ill. Clinical work is more closely scrutinized here than at any other time. Many different supervisors review virtually every decision made by the intern, from why it is necessary to set limits on a patient's freedom, to how to assess a thought disorder in an intake interview. Finally, supervisors must help to identify errors and problems in the intern's clinical practice and approach that need to be corrected or modified before the year ends.

The supervisory process requires tremendous patience from interns and supervisors. The intern begins the year as a student, and must end as a practitioner, nearly a colleague. In order to reach that level of competence a lot of mistakes are certain to be made by everybody. A working relationship must develop in which there is enough independence for honest mistakes, and yet enough restraint to prevent disasters.

Not every relationship between supervisor and intern is a

success—as in college, memorable students and teachers are few. The difference is that the internship is more invasive, the disasters potentially greater, and the disputes rarely neutral. For example, what is an intern supposed to do when a supervisor's approach to treatment differs radically from his own? And what can a supervisor do with an intern who consistently doesn't know how to listen to his patients?

My criteria for choosing an internship site were shaped by three teachers, whose advice, summed up, was that I try to get accepted as an intern to a public, in-patient facility (with an outpatient clinic attached to it, for follow-up care and emergency-room experience), that would be staffed by a major university, with an eclectic but psychodynamic orientation for teaching its psychology interns and psychiatry residents. They gave this advice to all their students.

My teachers felt that a public facility would provide me with an opportunity to work with a wide array of patients. I would learn about mentally ill people whose problems would be challenging on many levels due to their variety and complexity. The university staff would ensure that interns would be there primarily to learn, rather than merely to do drudgery. They would also be able to teach current theories and practices of psychotherapy, grounded in academic research. The eclectic approach would provide opportunities to learn different treatment modalities.

The guidance and care provided by my teachers—Bernie Green, Marv Hyman, James Keillor—proved to be extremely valuable. The choices facing me were confusing. There is no fixed sort of internship: one chooses from among a private outpatient clinic; a private in-patient hospital; an urban private practice; a public hospital serving the aged; a psychiatric wing of a public children's hospital; and so on. Theoretical orientation also varies from one setting to the next. Supervisors may be Freudian, behaviorists, psychodynamic, completely eclectic, and so on.

■   ■   ■   ■

In November of my final year of graduate course work, I applied to more than twenty-five internship programs; the typical number of applications sent out is under eight. I was a graduate student at the University of Detroit and was desperate to return East. Since internships are highly competitive, and my program was virtually unknown outside of Michigan, I figured my chances of acceptance would improve by tripling the number of applications. I *preferred* to work in an "in-patient, public hospital with university affiliation and an eclectic, psychodynamic teaching staff," but I was *willing* to accept almost any offer in the East in order to be closer to my girlfriend.

In December I interviewed at over a dozen sites in New England, most of them in the Hartford, Connecticut area, where my girlfriend lived, a few in Massachusetts. Initially, I did not take my interview in Boston at Commonwealth Mental Health Institute/Harvard Medical School as seriously as some others, because I doubted that I would be accepted there. It just seemed too prestigious a place; I assumed that they selected candidates only from famous graduate programs. I applied to Comm. Mental just to take a chance, like buying a state lottery ticket. As a result, I was less aware of my anxious feelings during the interview there than anywhere else.

The first interview at Comm. Mental was with Edith Katz, a staff psychologist. As was the case with interviewers at other internship sites, she asked me a combination of personal and professional questions: Was I in therapy? How was it going? What were my major issues? What issues did I feel interfered with my clinical work? Which sort of patients, diagnostically, did I feel most comfortable working with? Could I describe as close to verbatim as possible a recent therapy session I had conducted with a patient? Could I say a few words about my family?

Since I was used to this sort of intrusiveness by this time, I answered all her questions dutifully and with care. Edith must have enjoyed our conversation because abruptly she asked if I could stay an extra day to meet with Eli Schwartz, the director of the program. I saw my chance of acceptance go from long-shot to possible. She excused herself to call him. When Edith returned, it was to say that Eli was available the next morning.

Although he was very friendly, I remember only one question from my interview with Eli: Do you have a particular strength, outside of a clinical one, that you take pride in?

I told him that I have a good sense of direction. When I am in a strange city I always manage to find my way around. I can picture streets, and in this way, develop mental maps that enable me to reach destinations without having to ask passersby how to get there.

Eli smiled a lot and nodded his head up and down as he listened to my description of being independent enough to find my way. Harvard is filled with people who think of themselves as self-directed; I guess Eli saw my claim of having a good sense of direction as a metaphor for someone who knows where he is going. But who knows?

When I think about it now, my strength was also a weakness during the internship, and in all other important areas of my life at the time: I didn't know when to ask for help and persisted instead in taking my own path, even if I was unhappy or worried about being lost, and even if it was completely wrongheaded, just to avoid having to depend upon someone else's knowledge and support. My persistence caused me tremendous pain.

When I had completed all of my interviews, and reviewed all of my applications, Comm. Mental/Harvard Medical School became my first choice. Of all the sites I had applied to, the program had the best clinical, teaching, and research components. For example, the hospital has a population of patients who present with many types of disorders—schizophrenia, personality disorders, major affective disorders, seizure disorders, other neurological impairments, or some combination of these difficulties. In addition, psychology interns at Comm. Mental are given tremendous responsibility. They are treated, in most instances, as equals of the psychiatry residents in decision-making, treatment-planning, and case-load of patients. Also, a number of the psychiatrists and psychologists teaching there are internationally known for their original and thoughtful work with the mentally ill. They are scholars as well as superb clinicians. Their supervision is extremely focused and valuable. Finally, the topic of my doctoral thesis—the psychological effects of the nuclear threat upon adolescents—was being researched by psychiatrists affiliated with Harvard, and with luck, Comm. Mental's tie to the university would make it possible to meet and talk about our research.

On the second Monday in February, graduate students who have applied to internships wait to receive acceptance by telephone. The waiting may potentially end as late as noon the next day. A student has until that time to accept any offer.

By 10 A.M. on Monday, only one site had phoned to accept me. (I told them that I wasn't sure.) Then I sat in the kitchen, or paced the house, and waited. At two o'clock, I called Comm. Mental to tell Eli that if I was offered a position, I would take it. This was an unusual step to take; it is more common to wait for the call. I was feeling desperate. (Two other sites called that afternoon to offer acceptance; I still held out for Comm. Mental.) At four, Eli called back to accept me, and I was elated.

This book describes my psychology internship. It is divided into four sections. In the first section, I write about how Comm. Mental is organized, my initial contact with staff and fellow trainees, and some early work with patients. In the second section, I tell about four patients in the hospital's locked, in-patient unit for whose care I was primarily responsible during the internship. Their creativity, misery, hopelessness, contradictions, madness, and resilience are seen against the background of their confinement and treatment. In the third section, I write about supervision: a group for the psychology interns and psychiatry residents, individual supervision, and Eastmark, the hospital's out-patient/emergency room. In the last section, I describe termination with staff and patients.

Like many others, I started my internship on July 1st, and

it lasted until June 30th of the following year. The book follows this schedule and proceeds in a loose chronological way. All features of people in it have been altered or disguised to ensure confidentiality.

THE HOSPITAL

PRENTISS
HAS OUR ATTENTION
ON THE FIRST DAY

Prentiss has our attention. He is a bespectacled little man of medium height, and he looks rather like the CEO of a hygiene products corporation. He smiles often. His teeth are perfect. While he talks, Prentiss pauses dramatically, clasps his smooth hands, and turns to different parts of the room so that none of us feels left out. He is welcoming us to the Commonwealth Mental Health Institute, a state hospital that is also one of Harvard Medical School's fiefdoms in the city of Boston. (Harvard provides its teaching staff.) We are on our toes, leaning forward, in order to get a better glimpse of the man. Every word he says seems to resonate with potential meaning. We are that happy to be here. He pauses. In a moment, when he speaks, he will have my complete attention.

"Comm. Mental's reputation for excellence is based on its residency program, the quality of your supervisors, and the opportunity to use your learning to provide the best psychiatric care possible for your patients."

Unfortunately, Prentiss's little chat goes on in this vein for some time. It's not that he isn't pleasant; he's *very* pleasant. The problem is that he sounds like a public relations officer. He tells us things we could learn by reading a brochure. For example, that the hospital used to be called New England Psychopathic. That the plaques, paintings, and figureheads on the panelled walls around us represent past directors of the hospital. Psychiatry is a young profession, and so on. Then he tells us a few in-jokes. A clique of people laugh knowingly, and the rest of us grin because we sort of get the general outlines of what's supposed to be funny.

Just as he is nearing the end of his remarks, I realize that I have not been paying close enough attention to Prentiss. It's not what he says, but how he says it.

After all, it's not every day that Dr. Prentiss Cliff—director of Commonwealth Mental Health Institute; professor of psychiatry at Harvard Medical School; psychoanalyst at the Boston Psychoanalytic Institute; one of the chief powerbrokers of the psychiatric scene in Boston and, therefore, of the world—it's just not every day of the week that he will make time for you. Prentiss is an important and powerful man very used to being listened to and understood.

So if I am not getting something out of his introduction, I had better learn to tune in to his frequency. Make no mistake about it: this is his hospital. He is responsible. He runs the show. More specifically, he oversees its budgets, awards its contracts, has final say on the hiring of its teaching staff, and negotiates its funds.

Prentiss is, in fact, many things to many people. For us, he is our fearless leader who makes the rules. For the patients, he can be a frightening man whose decisions alter every aspect of their lives. We have more freedom than the mentally ill, but only as much as Prentiss will grant us.

Having made this point, Prentiss turns to the crowd and asks various people to introduce themselves.

Dr. Charles Hardwick, director of the psychiatry residency program, makes a few cheery remarks. Charles looks as if he has just stepped off a boat after a terrific day of sailing in Casco

Bay. He is tall, lean, tanned, and upbeat. If George Bush were a psychiatrist, he would look and sound like Charles Hardwick. A major difference, however: Hardwick is widely considered by the medical school's psychiatry department to be a genius. His book, *Integration of Pain,* is said to be brilliantly written. He talks like William F. Buckley, Jr. And he likes to say odd things that apparently have no association to one another until you think about them for a while.

Other illustrious names follow Hardwick: Abraham Heldeis, Fritz Pfefferman, Oliver Blaustein, Peter Mendelsohn. Each man is direct, articulate, well groomed, well dressed. The dress is casual, but conservative: white shirts, striped ties, khaki trousers, dark blazers, Wallabee shoes. The men look as if they are standing in a store window of Brooks Brothers.

And as with Dr. Cliff, it's not what they say, but how they say it. These men are, after all, his lieutenants. We get the impression quickly that while they don't hold as much power as the hospital director, they are powerful in other ways, ways we need to know about. For one thing, they seem to have no regrets about not being the director. They are apparently brilliant and accomplished in other areas. They make a pretense of disdaining political in-fighting. They imply that they are untainted by having to dicker with administrative issues. They are researchers, thinkers, explorers of the unconscious. Freudian to the man, they mean to understand the psyche!

We're all incredibly impressed by this presentation. In fact, most of us are overwhelmed. We look like a flock of ensnared birds giving up our souls to fate. Our eyes wander nervously. We stand on one foot, then another. We shift our weight. When we laugh, it is because we are nervous, not because what's said is particularly funny.

Our surroundings add to this feeling of tension. We're in the hospital's library, an extremely ornate affair of wood, glass, and marble. The bookshelves have glass doors. The card catalogues look as if they were made on special order. The door and window frames are a rich, syrupy color.

I feel as if I'm inside a private girl's school. I had a friend who attended Miss Porter's School for girls in Farmington, Connecticut, and the school offices where I waited for her looked like this. Naturally, the coffee table at Miss Porter's displayed copies of *The New Yorker* rather than *The Journal of the American Psychiatric Association,* but, overall, the library looks the same as the school: like a posh, exclusive club.

As I look around the room, listening casually to whichever famous, mellifluous speaker currently has the floor, allowing myself to feel relaxed by his elegance, I have to admit that I like it here. In fact, I like it a lot.

It's nice to be made to feel chosen. Not just anyone can become a psychology intern at this extremely prestigious institution. For years I have looked on Harvard with a mixture of envy and derision. To be invited in makes me feel proud. I also feel powerful. After all, if Prentiss and his lieutenants give us just a little bit of power we're way ahead of those on the outside. We feel special.

This feeling of entitlement isn't new for most of us assembled in the room. Prentiss and his staff are either Boston Brahmins, or, when they function as psychoanalysts, advisors to the Brahmins. And among the residents and interns, there are sons of millionaire businessmen, the daughter of a commercial airline pilot, lawyers' and physicians' sons and daughters, a film director's daughter, and the son of a psychologist. We have always been a privileged group. We feel destined to accomplish great things.

Since we're indebted to them for our presence in this room today, Prentiss and his colleagues will be able to manipulate as well as to guide us. We can feel the promise of more to come. We want badly to make the right impression and to be the best we can be partly in order to please them. We want to succeed according to their ideas of success.

I realize that I am starting to sound like the TV solicitations the Army uses to get ahold of recruits: "Be. Be all that you can be. You can do it. In the Army!"

It's no accident. The spirit of competitive militarism is in the air. Throughout the morning, I have heard talk of conquering affective disorders, siding with the defenses, and building alliances. We have met our leader and his men. (There are no women among Prentiss's lieutenants.) Most importantly, Harvard has assured us that our cause is a good one.

And, thus armed, we begin our tour of the hospital.

Before we start, however, some background on where we stand: Commonwealth Mental Health Institute is a rundown brick building located at 33 Boisvert Street. From the outside, it looks like an innovative prison. Metal bars are posted in the third-floor window frames. Plump security guards, one wearing glittering chains around his neck, patrol its grounds.

The hospital is part of a huge medical complex that includes Harvard Medical School, Mt. Zion Hospital, the Muhlenberg Cancer Institute, The Family Institute, Baskin Women's Hospital, and the Leopoldstadt.

Before this area became world-renowned for its medical services, it was a quiet, working-class neighborhood called Mission Hill. Mission Hill still exists in truncated form. Many of the residents, according to stories that have appeared in *The Boston Globe*, are angry with Harvard. They feel that Harvard is insensitive to their concerns. They don't want Harvard to continue its invasion of their neighborhood.

Standing before Comm. Mental, you'd never guess that a neighborhood with any cohesion ever existed here. Disheveled people pace the front sidewalk. They wear shabby clothes and talk about God and Satan. It's clear to see that they feel possessed by visions and hear voices that make them feel helpless and afraid. Much of their disadvantage, their despair often has a comical quality to it. They talk about things normal people dream about. They say whatever comes into their heads. They don't care about logical sequence in a conversation. They have a private understanding of time.

When you cross the threshold of the hospital, you enter its lobby. More patients wander and stumble about here. Recently, the hospital administration had all the couches taken out of the lobby to discourage loitering. Now the patients pace the long, dimly lit hallways, sit on the stairs, or assemble behind the staff's kitchen. As they rock, stare into space, or smoke cigarette after cigarette, they acquire a vacant, passive look.

I have seen that look before on the numbed faces of people in the Third World who sit in shabby terminals waiting for buses. In Oaxaca, Mexico, I watched a man stand in line to buy a ticket to go north where there was work. I learned from him that he had waited all day long. When he finally reached the ticket window, he was told that all seats for the next month had been sold. He didn't react at all, not even with a gesture. He simply walked out of the station.

That's how most mental patients look. The hopelessness which they endure is so familiar to them, and so ancient a feeling, that any small change in their lives necessitates a revolutionary break with the past. The break feels radical to them because despite the fact that the past haunts them, it is all they have to anchor them to life. They are numb to experience because their involvement with others, and with the world, has been empty. They wander through the hospital like the corpses in *Night of the Living Dead*.

As we tour the chapel, gym, administrative offices, kitchen, yard, and lounges, a few of these people make strong impressions. For example, there is Jimmy, a frail, balding wisp of a man who never stands up straight. We learn that he is always begging for change. When he gets enough money, he buys himself a cheeseburger at the staff kitchen. When he finishes eating, he has a smoke. Then he begs for more change. This goes on all day, day after day. To add to the tragedy, it is common knowledge in the hospital that until his mother's death ten years ago, Jimmy was a brilliant violinist. It is rumored that all of his former genius is dissipated, except for his ability to play an unbeatable game of chess.

Another man who is like a fixture in and around the hospital is an extremely tall, gaunt, bald man with no teeth, whose mouth looks like a gash, and who walks in a sort of crouch clutching a naked Barbie doll. Due to his prodigious size, one expects to hear him speak gruffly, but instead he talks in a very high falsetto like a cartoon baby.

The Priest is also well known. Never seen in anything but his vestments, the Priest blesses everyone he meets. One hand makes the sign of the cross, the other clutches a cigarette with dangling ash. Last week the Priest was placed in seclusion because he became uncontrollably violent in his refusal to take medication.

Compared to Jimmy, the Priest, and the other stragglers, our assembly of ten psychiatry residents, six psychology interns, and several staff psychiatrists looks like manikins. We're clean-cut, calm, and thoughtful. I feel like a reluctant missionary sent to civilize the natives. My sympathies lie with the victims of progress. I'm not convinced that we know enough about their world to change or tame it. I am more interested in understanding the madness than in trying to make it disappear.

As our journey continues, I meet the staffs of day hospital one, where I have been assigned, and of the locked in-patient unit. Two interns and five residents are assigned to each of the two day hospitals. (In addition to our duties on the day hospital, we carry a caseload of about eight in-patients.) The day hospital is an 8:30 A.M.–3:30 P.M. treatment facility. Most of the forty-five patients here began their hospitalizations on the in-patient unit. As their symptoms of psychiatric illness became less noticeable and destructive, and as they became easier to manage, they were shifted to the day hospital.

The day-hospital program is based on the idea of milieu therapy. (Milieu therapy works on the principles that staff creates a milieu in which therapy goes on all the time in many different settings within the day hospital.) Patients are required to participate in a wide variety of group activities, including warm-up, community meeting, group therapy, and wrap-up. In addition, depending on what their needs are perceived to be, they are assigned by their treatment team to movement therapy, baking group, arts group, or transition group. Each treatment team consists of a psychiatry resident, psychology intern, social worker, mental health assistant, and nurse.

The nurses on day hospital one and the in-patient unit are: Dolly, Christina, Betty Anne, Kate, Ellen, and Maura. Dolly, the day hospital's head nurse, is a woman in her late forties. She looks like Mrs. Bartle, my kindergarten teacher. She speaks softly and simply, using few words to express many complex thoughts. As I get to know her, I learn that Dolly never expresses her anger openly. If she is upset about something, she says, "I guess I feel that a mistake was made." Dolly refers to herself and the other nurses as "the girls."

The nurses act jolly and confident when we meet on the in-patient unit to exchange greetings. They are not assured of their power like Prentiss and his lieutenants. Most of them grew up in Irish working-class neighborhoods of Boston. Each year they provide the nitty-gritty orientation for a fresh crop of interns and residents, and it is clear to see that they are mildly amused by our intensity and confusion; they smirk at our clean-cut appearances.

Similarly amused are the mental health assistants, known as M.H.A.'s. They are muscular black men called Anton, Sonny, Rashid, and Frank. They never talk much. They are on the units to protect the nurses, to prevent violence from occurring or escalating, and to talk to the patients. They encourage patients to take their medicine. They play Scrabble with them in the sitting rooms. During a code green, which is a general alarm sounded in the hospital when a patient has become violent, they take leading roles in subduing the threat.

Even in our orientation, we have an opportunity to witness a problem being solved by the M.H.A.'s and the nurses. A patient has chosen to interrupt our meeting. The patient is Mary Donahue, a mildly retarded, plump individual in her late teens who carries a diagnosis of chronic, undifferentiated schizophrenia. Mary has been in and out of hospitals since her childhood. Ever since she can remember, she has heard voices telling her to hurt herself and others. She cannot read or write. She was sexually molested by her father. Her family never comes to visit her. Mary has a reputation for violent behavior. Every now and then she punches out a window.

"Hey, Betty Anne, what's going on?"

"Mary, we're in the middle of a meeting." Betty Anne, who is a year or two older than Mary, sounds as if she's trying to lull a child to sleep. Her tone is even and calm. "I can't talk to you right now."

"Aw, come on, you promised. You promised you'd call welfare for me. You promised!"

"Mary, after the meeting's over, I'll talk to you, OK?"

"And when's that gonna be?"

Betty Anne looks at her watch and says, looking up, "Twenty minutes."

"I can't wait that long!"

Betty Anne looks over to Sonny. He gets up, sucks in his gut, takes Mary by the elbow, and quietly starts to lead her away.

"Let's go," he says.

Mary argues with him and starts to cry.

"No one loves me!"

She is a sight, this big, bawling, delusional teenager resisting the strength of the M.H.A.'s grip on her. She won't give in. She wants her nurse.

"Betty Anne!"

Betty Anne excuses herself to talk with Mary. They walk up and down the corridor of the unit. I can hear them whispering. When Mary calms down, Betty Anne rejoins our group.

"What a baby," she whispers to us with a conspiratorial giggle. "You have to set limits with them. That's one of the first things you'll need to learn about working here."

When the meeting ends, I watch a man being brought in on a stretcher. He is black and bearded. He wears an earring that is really a brooch that spells "Nancy." He is tied to the stretcher and doesn't like it. He struggles against his straps.

Three M.H.A.'s and three security guards carry the stretcher and deposit it and the man on the sticky floor of a seclusion room—the place where admissions felt to be dangerous are locked up in order to contain and isolate them completely from the community. They kneel beside him.

"One! Two! Three!"

At the end of the count, the straps holding the man are undone. Freed at last, he tries to rush forward, to sit, perhaps eventually to stand. The men guarding him know his plan. They flip him over on his belly.

"Rape!" he cries.

They pull down his pants, and while they try to hold him still, a psychiatrist shoots him up with an injection of Haldol. Haldol is a powerful antipsychotic medicine that serves as a tranquilizer. Having accomplished their mission, the M.H.A.'s, the guards, and the doctor scurry to exit the seclusion room. They make it out just in time. The patient runs after them, but winds up facing a locked door.

This locked door has a tiny, rectangular observation window about six inches long and two inches wide. The patient has backed away and is standing in the center of the seclusion room. I observe him.

First, he unzips his fly, takes out his penis, and pees on the floor. Then he steps to the other end of the room and begins to perform martial arts exercises. He pulls back the string of a hunters' bow. He steps over a narrow abyss. He evades a blow. The motions are angular and furious. He looks like a praying mantis. He preens himself, flexes his muscles, and makes his hands into fists.

Betty Anne taps me on the shoulder.

"Congratulations." She hands me a manila file folder. "He's yours. The cops say his name is John Plummer. He's crazy as a bedbug, isn't he? Needs lots of meds. Hope he's not violent, but Flanagan [the security chief] says he's got a black belt in karate."

Although Mr. Plummer is secluded, I still have to do an intake interview with him. This interview helps determine the admission's mental status, educational and occupational status, medical history, social history, and psychiatric history. I learn about these determinants when I ask Christina what I am supposed to find out in an intake. I have never done one before. Mr. Plummer is my first in-patient.

My ignorance is pretty typical for a psychology intern. Psychologists are not customarily an integral part of in-patient psychiatric treatment facilities. It's a turf issue, and the psychiatrists have won. The residents already know how to write orders in the order book, "do" a mental status, and get a history. Initially, psychologists don't. We are not trained medically, and therefore cannot function with ease in a medical hospital. To our advantage, however, we have treated a good number of the mentally ill as out-patients, while the psychiatry residents have rarely treated anyone who is strictly in need of psychological care.

How did the psychiatrists win the right to establish the guidelines for treatment of the mentally ill? In a mental hospital the hierarchy of power is: psychiatrist, psychologist, social worker, nurse, mental health assistant. In the medical world, in contrast, psychiatrists do not have the same high status.

Psychiatry's successful grab for power in the field of mental health is probably a response to their low position among fellow physicians. And the nature of their assertiveness is part of that response. They seek to demonstrate that medical science, as opposed to psychological theory, best explains human behavior. They want to show that they are physicians as well as healers of the psyche. For example, modern psychiatry relies heavily upon biochemistry and genetics to explain the complex phenomena of schizophrenia, major affective disorders, and alcoholism. Medication for mania, major depression, and psychosis is the rule rather than the exception. When patients complain about the side effects of neuroleptic medications—impotence, tardive dyskinesia (an irreversible condition consisting of repeated grimacing of the mouth and facial muscles), stiffness, a numb experience of clouded thoughts—they are routinely told that medication will ease their suffering despite its drawbacks. Often, a patient's reluctance to take medication is interpreted as resistance to treatment.

Overall, psychotherapy is seen as adjunctive to the psychopharmacological treatment of schizophrenia and the other major psychiatric disorders. The so-called talking cure has gone a little bit out of fashion because its results—its cure rate—are judged

by academic researchers and federal and private grant founda-
tions to be poor. (Psychotherapy defies a systematic approach to
mental illness.) It is tragic that the importance of forming a
relationship with the patient has been devalued in the treatment
of the profoundly mentally ill.

The business of classifying disorders is also one of psychiatry's contributions to the field of mental health. The phenomenon of suffering now has its own nosology. *The Diagnostic
and Statistics Manual of Mental Disorders (Third Edition) Re-
vision (DSM-III-R)* offers five axes that chart behavioral mani-
festations, duration of illness, level of functioning, recurrence,
range of affect, orientation, and so on. *DSM-III-R* permits many
people of diverse philosophies regarding treatment to use a single diagnostic term they can all agree upon to describe a complex phenomenon.

In addition to *DSM-III-R,* modern psychiatry uses jargon to
describe the experience of madness. The technical language is
comprehensible primarily to an elite. For example, instead of
saying "A woman has visions of doom," we can now say she
has "auditory hallucinations which limit ego functioning." Instead of saying "A man has always been lonely," we can now
say that he has "poor object relations." Instead of saying that
it is frightening and confusing to sit with lonely people who have
visions of doom, we can now say that "the phenomenon of
countertransference needs to be interpreted in order to analyze
its role in the therapeutic alliance."

Psychiatry's control of the field of mental health is taken
for granted. It does not come under scrutiny. This is a hospital,
and we play by their rules. And so, despite my misgivings about
doing an intake, I enter Mr. Plummer's cage. Anton accompanies me as protection.

"Mr. Plummer, I'm Dr. Haas." Thomas ("Tom") Downes,
the psychiatrist super-chief of day hospital one, has instructed
me to use the title of doctor even though I am only a doctoral
candidate. The psychiatry residents *are* doctors, and Tom feels
that we should all call ourselves doctors in order to avoid confusing the patients. I don't agree with Tom's reasoning, but com-

ply with it. For one thing, I like the status of the title even though I don't deserve it.

"Mr. Plummer? I need to ask you some questions. Is that OK?"

"Don't ask him if it's OK," says Anton.

"Mr. Plummer?"

Mr. Plummer is sitting on the floor, his face to the wall. I kneel just out of his arm's reach.

"Mr. Plummer?"

He ignores me. I start to sweat because I imagine that any second I am going to get clobbered. Fortunately, my fantasy isn't shared by Mr. Plummer. He just stares away. He's in another world.

"Mr. Plummer?"

I begin to wonder what world he's in. I try to think of some mutual reference point. What can I ask him about that won't seem threatening? What do we share as people? All I can think of is his loss of freedom. I feel sorry for Mr. Plummer. I empathize with his feeling of humiliation. How can I help him?

"You should ask him where he lives," says Anton. He can't believe that I'm not yet inured to this hellish place. "Maybe he's not in this catchment area."

A catchment area is the zone of residency for a state hospital. If Mr. Plummer lives outside of our zone, he will be sent to the state facility that provides care to his area.

"I don't think he'll tell me."

"Are you afraid?" asks Anton. "Don't be afraid. That's why I'm here."

We converse in front of Mr. Plummer as if he's a piece of furniture. The room smells of urine. The stained mattress on the floor looks as if it's been taken from a Bolivian prison.

I decide to ask all my required questions, and to proceed even if I don't get any answers.

"Mr. Plummer, how old are you?"

Silence.

"When's your birthday? Where do you live? Do you have

sisters and brothers? Are you married? Are your parents living?
What are their names?''

We are a sad sight, me, Anton, and Mr. Plummer huddled
in this tiny room failing to make contact. It's as if we are three
fallen aliens, with our only shared experience the isolation we
suffer from one another.

"Ask him proverbs," suggests Anton.

"Mr. Plummer, what does the saying 'strike while the iron
is hot' mean?''

At the end of my twenty-minute interview, I know as much
about John Plummer as I did before I stepped into the seclusion
room. His failure to talk to me results in a blank intake sheet.
Tom mildly criticizes me for my inability to take an adequate
history and suggests talking with Mr. Plummer tomorrow morning when he has adjusted to his hospitalization.

When the next day comes, however, Mr. Plummer is gone.
He recovered enough to be freed from seclusion and placed in
the locked in-patient sitting room. For a while, he stood around
smoking cigarettes. He quietly accepted five-minute checks.
These checks are imposed on patients who are felt to be at great
risk of being a threat to themselves or to others. Every five minutes an M.H.A. checks up on them.

But Mr. Plummer's submission turns out to have been
surface-deep. When Betty Anne unlocked the unit's door with a
huge iron skeleton key, he hurled her out of the way and made
his escape. He ran down the stairs, out a side door of the hospital, and into the street.

We think we're free of him, but two weeks later Mr. Plummer is brought back in by the Boston police. This time he has
shaved his head and is dressed as if he's just stepped out of the
pages of *Gentleman's Quarterly.* He asks to be called Dr. Plummer. He says that he's a world-famous professor of "pediatric
medical surgery." He lectures to the nurses when they tell him
it's time to take his medication. And when the two of us are
alone, he begins to tell me the truth.

THERE IS NEVER
ENOUGH TIME

There is never enough time to see things through. I run a therapy group in the day hospital at the same time that I am expected to attend the case conference in the locked in-patient unit. I have supervision (eight hours each week) by teaching staff of my clinical cases when I need to be at community meeting. (During supervision we go over, sometimes word for word, critically, the content of my therapy sessions with in-patients in order to improve my work with them.) When I see day-hospital patients for therapy, I neglect out-patients and in-patients. And when there is an emergency involving any of my patients (in-, out-, or day-hospital), I must drop whatever I am doing and attend to the problem at once. All of the interns and residents suffer from the same conflict of schedule, and we complain about it constantly.

At the same time, our griping has a gleeful, noble, and competitive quality. For although we have lost most of our free time to read, write, think clearly, or simply play, we take pride in our machinelike ability to work hard. From our tone, we could be talking about sports. Or we could be talking about how good we think we are.

Who worked the greatest number of hours last week? How many? Fifty? Sixty? Seventy? We share several assumptions: the harder we work, the more we know. We know what we're doing. We are very important. The work is meaningful.

The hospital administration does little to discourage our foolishness. Why should they? Charles Hardwick, et al., are reputed to put in fourteen-hour days. There is certainly work that needs to be done. No one is putting in long hours in order to count paper clips.

But what we lose by working too hard is some of the capacity to meditate on our patients. I don't have time to be very curious about Mr. Plummer, for example. I can register the shock I felt when I first saw him brutalized. I can begin to form a diagnosis and treatment plan. But to think about him as a genuine person, with loves, sorrows, memories, losses, and desires, feels frightening.

Frightening? I didn't mean to use that word. I was complaining about the schedule. And what's fear got to do with that? Nothing.

Then is there something else behind my feeling of being overworked? Am I blaming the hectic pace for stirring up fear that, in fact, already exists? Do I try to lose myself in the schedule to avoid confronting this shameful feeling?

I try to dismiss it, but then I begin to wonder why I am afraid of someone who comes to me for help. I feel overwhelmed during conversations with Mr. Plummer, but what is it precisely that feels burdensome? When I first met with him, I was frightened by his helpless condition. As he struggled against the doctor and M.H.A.'s, I wished that magically he would become better. It scared me to think he might not improve very much at all. As I wondered about his future, I began to experience the hopelessness he must feel most of the time. It felt intolerable.

It scares me when I have to tolerate sadness and pain that cannot be quickly assuaged. Faced with profound sorrow, I feel pressed to *do* something or *say* something—when there's nothing to be said or done. After all, before I say or do anything, I have to learn to sit in a room alone with this man without feeling frightened or estranged. And without being preoccupied by my feeling of anxiety; rather, I must observe quietly his presence and acknowledge his needs. Why can't I simply listen to Mr. Plummer talk about himself?

I wonder if I'll be able to be of any use to him. Not only must I make time to see him more often, but when we are together I have to find things we have in common. I must approach him with stealth and patience. If he cannot conceal his suffering, I must not hide my love.

And yet there is so much work to do that takes me away from him and the others in the locked unit.

Most of my time is spent in the day hospital. I see seven day-hospital patients for therapy, run or attend two day-hospital groups, and work in my office in the day hospital. There are two day hospitals at Comm. Mental, and both are located on the building's third floor, divided by a stairwell and a pair of clunky elevators.

About forty-five patients attend each day hospital. A few are quartered in the locked in-patient unit, but most are living in halfway houses, at home with their parents, in boarding-houses, in nursing homes, in shelters (for example, the Boisvert Inn, a dormitory for homeless patients), set up in the hospital's gym, in federal housing projects, or in apartments. Few patients own any property, to say nothing of their own homes.

Our day hospital consists of a long L-shaped corridor with two sitting rooms and offices all along the way. Patients hang out in the sitting rooms when they don't have a scheduled activity. The main room has two or three broken couches; a folding table; some old kitchen chairs; crude, handmade wooden cabinets containing board games, jigsaw puzzles, and used paperbacks; a few posters of sunsets, sunrises, mountains, oceans, Garfield the cartoon cat, or puppies fighting; and a wall-length week's schedule of activities going on in the day hospital.

The offices lining the corridor are occupied by two psychology interns, two psychiatry residents, social workers, nurses, and occupational therapy (better known as o.t.). This design of placing clinicians in the treatment setting leads to the broader concept of milieu therapy. Instead of limiting benefits to one-to-one contact, milieu therapy seeks to establish a therapeutic atmosphere.

To foster the process of a milieu, the day hospital seeks active group participation. The one group led by patients is community meeting, held twice weekly for a half-hour. Community meeting is the largest group activity in the day hospital because everyone is required to attend.

The patients make up the agenda for community meetings and chair these gatherings (with an occasional assist from Jamie Armstrong, Carol Silber, or Amy Bond, social workers). The principal item on the agenda is the topic for discussion. Before each community meeting, a patients' committee selects a topic. Their selection is based on a variety of factors, including informal surveys they've taken of their fellow patients. Recent topics have included: "Is it OK to get angry at your doctor?"; "The pros and cons of taking medication"; and "Is staff available when you need them?"

At today's meeting, Bill, an emaciated ex-boxer, complained about the staff's overreliance upon interpretation. What he wanted was empathy. The topic was: "Does staff understand patients' needs?"

"If I tell my doctor I'm angry," he says, "he says that underneath it all, I'm sad. But if I tell him that I'm depressed, he says underneath it all I'm angry. Do any of the doctors really know what they're talking about? Why do we listen to their crap?"

Reactions of staff and patients vary at community meetings, of course, but some factors are constant. For one thing, our group of interns and residents moves stiffly. I move my body as if I suffer partial paralysis from the neck down. And like my colleagues, my voice sounds tender, but unreal. I try to soothe with my voice. Instead, I sound like the ubiquitous Mrs. Bartle, my kindergarten teacher.

I find myself saying "I guess I feel" a lot.

"I guess I feel that you're saying that your doctor isn't helping you.

"I guess I feel that you're saying that staff has to do more than try and name your feelings.

"I guess I feel like you're pretty upset."

Our formality, so different from the intimacy of our private sessions, is met by a customarily docile bunch turned into a community with shared values. At today's meeting, which was typical, they shout one another down, tell jokes, and clamor for attention. Several people seize the floor at various times to make impassioned pleas.

Although their threats never get out of hand, we are disturbed by the display. In our offices, behind closed doors, fantasies, theirs and ours, seem more manageable. But during this meeting the boundaries between patient and clinician open somewhat. We become members of the same community, and although clinicians hold more power, the kinship between those who suffer and those who heal becomes apparent. Much to my detriment, I react to this proximity by trying to hide myself. And because the day is crammed with activities, I can make no more than a note of my odd behavior. (An example of how a crowded day serves as a defense against anxiety.)

Two other activities requiring participation of all day-hospital patients are warm-up and wrap-up. Similar to home-room in many high schools, warm-up, the day's first activity, sets up seven or eight people with a supervisor who checks attendance and for signs of disturbance that might worsen as the day progresses. In the day hospital, the groups are led by nurses. Wrap-up, the day's final activity, returns each group to the same nurse with whom they started the day.

Each intern and resident is required to lead at least one group. The resident may choose virtually any subject for a group; the intern must run a therapy group. The residents' groups include juggling, art appreciation, and transition, which deals with the problems of making the transition from hospitalization to freedom.

I lead a therapy group and a creative writing group. The therapy group meets twice weekly in my office for forty-five minutes each session. My co-leader is Ellen Wilson, a day-hospital nurse. We have between three and eight patients in our group. Among the regulars are Bob and Mr. Kingston, two older white men who sit stiffly and say nothing. Mr. Kingston has aristocratic pretensions. He alone, of all the day-hospital patients, is never referred to by his first name. He always sits with angular bearing, his chin up as far as it will go.

Mr. Kingston's self-righteous stares often inhibit group conversation. Ellen and I have made our edict: talk about your feelings! But with a stern grandfather type present, progress is slow.

A more critical problem is poor attendance. It's very unusual if everyone shows up to two consecutive meetings. As a result, topics and problems are not carried over from week to week. Each session stands by itself.

Mr. Kingston, Bob, Darlene, Howie, and Dennis attended today's meeting. In contrast to Mr. Kingston and Bob, Darlene, Howie, and Dennis are in their twenties or thirties, high-spirited, active, humorous, and hopeful. They are hopeful primarily because they have not suffered for a long time yet. They still think that their predicaments may be temporary. There is more resilience in young people with disorders because the disruptions in their functioning due to mental illness have not yet become as familiar to them as daybreak, which is often the case in the older, chronic patient. (All five group members carry psychiatric diagnoses between them that indicate severe mental illness: schizophrenia, [chronic, undifferentiated type]; manic-depression; schizophrenia, [paranoid type]).

The meetings begin after everyone, except for me, hauls chairs from a sitting room into my office. A circle is formed with the chairs. Then we sit around until someone has something "to share with the group." Private conversations are forbidden. Verbal participation is encouraged, but not strictly required.

Dennis, a young white man who was admitted last week to

the locked in-patient unit, entertains us with blues songs he composed after spending time in the mental hospital. Darlene, a nineteen-year-old from posh suburbs whose parents are teaching her a lesson by not sending her to a private hospital, encourages him, and they sing together for a while. Howie, a manic-depressive with several years of college-level psychology courses under his belt, objects.

"Dr. Haas," he says with a sneer, "do you really think this is useful? Is this why we're required to come to group? To listen to people making displays of themselves?"

"What's on your mind?"

"Well, for one thing, I don't think those assholes—oops, excuse me, I mean the psychiatrists—know what they're doing. I'm not blaming you, Dr. Haas, because you're a psychologist. Some people know the difference."

"What's your objection to the psychiatrists? I still don't know what it is you're objecting to."

"That's because I haven't told you yet. I thought psychologists were trained to listen. Or am I thinking of psychiatrists? I don't know." He grins like the Cheshire cat. "Anyway, I don't belong here is the point. I have manic-depressive illness. My doctor told me. And I looked it up, I've been studying it, in fact, and it seems that manic-depressive illness is a biochemical imbalance which improves with lithium. In fact, symptoms can disappear completely with the use of that drug. To be perfectly honest, Dr. Haas, I wouldn't act crazy anymore if I took lithium. But the descriptions of treatment of manic-depression say nothing about the so-called benefits of psychotherapy. And so I've agreed to take the lithium, *if* I don't have to attend the day hospital. So why do I still have to attend the day hospital? It doesn't help me at all. I'm being held here against my will. I'm being blackmailed by my doctor."

My first comment: "How is he blackmailing you?"

"He won't let me take the lithium unless I attend the day hospital."

My last comment: "And you don't think the day hospital is helpful so you refuse to cooperate fully with your doctor."

Because I didn't understand very much of what Howie was trying to convey to me symbolically, my comments did not affect him. I have to learn to say nothing if I have nothing to say. But I get anxious with dead air. Before I can explore what my anxiety is about, Ellen, who has heard Howie's story before and knows what is going on, responds.

"Howie, you bring this up in group every week, and every week people try to talk to you about what's going on with you emotionally, but you won't listen to them."

"What's going on with *you* emotionally?"

"Howie, I'm serious! If you want to know why you're in the day hospital, bring it up with your doctor. If you want to participate in group, then participate in group."

Meanwhile, I have just noticed that Mr. Kingston is getting pissed-off with Dennis and Darlene. He shifts from his seated, statuelike pose. He fidgets. He touches an eyebrow, tugs at an earlobe, sits on his hands, clutches the chair, rocks forward nearly an inch, and then clears his throat.

"Mr. Kingston, is something upsetting you?"

"Well, yes," he says, keeping his head perfectly still, "yes, indeed. I'm sorry, but disrespectful singing filled with obscene language just isn't my cup of tea. At all."

"Disrespectful? Hey, OK," says Dennis suddenly. "Jeez, I didn't know. Hey, if my singing bothers you, no problem. Just say the word and I'll quit it. I'm not like some guys who can't take a hint. Just tell me to stop doing something and I'll quit doing it. I hate being a nuisance. My mother says my problem all along has been not knowing when to leave people alone. I've always been kind of a jerk-off. And you know what's weird? What's weird is I don't even like being around people that much. I mean, isn't that weird?"

Darlene laughs and looks at her hands, folded in her lap like petals.

"That's OK," says Mr. Kingston, still keeping his chin up, "that's quite OK."

It's not easy for any of the patients in the group to make conversation. They are not used to being understood, or even heard, and after a while they stop trying. Then they begin to forget what it's like to talk to another human being. This process of forgetting fits in with the day hospital's program of expressive groups, which make use of abilities besides that of speech. One important aim of the program is to find ways for disconnected people to form relationships.

For example: the creative writing group meets once a week for forty-five minutes. It is an elective for both me and the patients. Our meetings vary. Sometimes we read from a published poet; at other times patients read from their own work (written during the week, or on the spot); and, now and then, we write a poem as a group. Our reading is eclectic and has included Robert Lowell, Theodore Roethke, Delmore Schwartz, Rainer Maria Rilke, and Villon. I usually choose the poet, because no one else offers any suggestions. Most often Wilma, an ex-actress who was a member of a prestigious repertory company in New York, reads.

Today Wilma read "The Heavy Bear Who Goes With Me," by Delmore Schwartz. My favorite lines in the poem refer to the longings of the bear accompanying Schwartz wherever he goes, and how the bear, ". . . Howls in his sleep for a world of sugar, /A sweetness intimate as the water's clasp."

The patients appreciate the poem in different ways.

"I think of the bear as a symbol of sadness," says Darlene, of the suburbs and therapy group. "Or he could be symbolic of lust, or of inner, weighty things."

"Or he might be a secret shadow," offers Wilma.

To prevent the group from turning into a comparative literature seminar, I also encourage patients to write and read their own work. After a poem is read, group members offer their reactions. In contrast to many groups of nonhospitalized writers, the reactions in this group are customarily positive. The main thing seems to be to offer support for another's effort to be understood.

Their poetry differs from that of nonpsychiatric individuals in several ways. For one thing, it is more intense. Nothing is taken lightly. Every object that interests them resonates with highly idiosyncratic meanings.

At the same time, emotional experiences between group members occur without strict reference to the past, present, and future. This makes it difficult to understand how relationships evolve between them. As a result, the boundaries between fantasy and reality open. The language employed is passionate and unintentionally surreal; it reflects, I believe, both their internal organization of perceived events and the real conditions they face in the mental hospital. All of the participants in the creative writing group have been through the humiliation of extended locked in-patient hospitalizations. They know what it's like to lose control, and the language they use reflects that loss.

With the exception of supervision and out-patient work, most of my time outside the day hospital is spent in the locked in-patient unit upstairs. The patients admitted to this unit are usually brought in by the local police. They are evaluated at Comm. Mental's out-patient unit, Eastmark Clinic, which is located on the ground floor. In order to be admitted as a patient to the locked in-patient unit, individuals must be either suicidal, homicidal, or unable to take adequate care of themselves due to a major mental illness that can best be treated within a mental hospital. Milieu therapy does not apply to this unit: it is designed to be a temporary holding area, a place for patients until they are seen to be well enough to participate in the day-hospital program downstairs.

One reason that the conditions for admission are strict is because the locked in-patient unit's census is usually high. There is room for about thirty-two people, but the census is often pushing forty. This means that there are not enough beds. There are dormitory-style bedrooms, but several people have to sleep on couches in the unit's two dayrooms. They wake up in pajamas or rumpled clothing, surrounded by staff and other groggy patients.

The dayrooms serve as the unit's town squares. They are

dirty, noisy, and crowded. It's almost impossible to engage in private behavior. There are few scheduled activities, so the patients hang out here all day. Most of them do nothing but sit mutely in a chair, smoke cigarettes, and jerk their arms or legs back and forth. (Their muscular spasms are sometimes a side effect of their medication.) A few watch TV. Some play Ping-Pong with an M.H.A. Now and then, a gin game gets started. The one telephone the patients may receive outside calls on is located in the front dayroom. (Patients with phone privileges are permitted to make outside calls using this phone.)

Patients also meet with their doctors in the dayrooms. Intake interviews and therapy sessions usually take place with patient and doctor sitting side by side on an old couch while other patients interrupt or mill about. The alternatives for talking with patients are limited to the seclusion room or a bedroom, if a patient has one. All of the professional offices are either in the day hospital or elsewhere in the hospital. The lack of privacy, especially in a society that cherishes the allure of private behavior, can contribute to the patient's feeling of being exposed.

A recent admission, Mr. Anastasi, an ex-factory worker in his late twenties, allowed himself to be interviewed by me in the dayroom. While we speak, the TV shows cartoons, nurses call out people's names for medications, and other interns and residents sit with other patients all around the room. We, the interviewers, look like Mormons talking to those we feel are in need of faith. We wear good, clean clothes, carry books, and speak quietly with some assurance. The patients wear dirty old clothes, usually have nothing except loose change, and mutter responses to the general inquiry.

The questions in an intake interview, designed to get as much pertinent background information as possible on an individual in a very limited time, are intrusive and difficult to answer even under the best circumstances. I ask Mr. Anastasi whether he knows his address, phone number, birthdate, and age. I ask him if he's ever been hospitalized before, whether he uses medication, alcohol, or illegal drugs. I ask him if he finished school, found a job, got married, and had a family. I ask him if his parents and siblings are healthy. I ask him if he hears voices.

Most of my questions are met with grunts, monosyllabic replies, or silent stares. His stares frighten me because Mr. Anastasi is a big man with a reputation for having a bad temper. During our interview, his eyes cloud and his jaw muscles clench.

Mr. Anastasi's background helps explain his predicament. He was transferred to Comm. Mental from Monterey State Hospital, a locked facility for the criminally insane. He had been arrested for a minor criminal offense, then found to be too crazy to serve time in prison.

Inmates at Monterey are said to be a recalcitrant lot, too crazy for prison but too violent for a mental hospital.

After serving time there and doing well, Mr. Anastasi is being given a chance to return to society. His return will be gradual. If he stays out of trouble on the locked in-patient unit, he will be transferred to the day hospital. If he does well at the day hospital, he will become an out-patient. Mr. Anastasi, although he has not been cooperative with me, has made it known that he is eager to return home.

Unfortunately, Mr. Anastasi has decompensated during his first week on the locked in-patient unit. This means that his personal hygiene has worsened, his clothing is disheveled, his manner has become intermittently odd and then withdrawn. He doesn't express himself clearly. Specifically, he accuses the doctors at Monterey of lying to him about the process of becoming reintegrated into society. He acts deeply suspicious. He has been caught drinking men's cologne.

"The doctors at Monterey told me that when I left that place I could go home. Now you tell me I have to stay locked up in here until you decide I'm ready to leave. And I can't even leave because first I got to go to the day hospital, whatever that is. I'll tell you, I would've never left Monterey if I knew you guys were going to put me through all this red tape. At least there we got to go for walks and stuff. I'm stuck in this place twenty-four hours a day. It's worse than prison."

I have had problems interviewing Mr. Anastasi because I keep feeling that he's going to reach over and clobber me. I stutter and sweat when I sit beside him. I find it difficult to maintain eye contact. Because I'm frightened, Tom Downes assists in the interview process. Tom is a small, very polite man with thin hair, many pastel-colored suits, and a characteristic grin. Although he is soft-spoken, he manages to create the impression that he is always aware of what's going on.

"We can appreciate your situation, Mr. Anastasi," he says, "but you have to understand that in order for us to do what you want, you have to show us that you're ready to go to day hospital. Dr. Haas and I don't feel you're ready to come downstairs. We feel that we need to get to know you better."

He glowers at Tom and lights up a Marlboro.

"I don't belong in a mental hospital. 'Cause I'm not nuts, OK? I broke the law and I did my time and now I want to go home. And if you can't find anything wrong with me, then I want to go home."

"We can't let you go home until we know more about you."

Mr. Anastasi looks away slowly. When he turns back, his eyelids are lowered and his lips are twisted to show his disgust.

"Mr. Anastasi?"

"I got nothing more to say to you."

He puts his hands on his knees, and then he rises.

"OK, Mr. Anastasi," says Tom, still seated. "Thank you for speaking to us."

"What do you think?" I ask.

"Well, I can see where he can be frightening," whispers Tom. He smiles and shoots a look to the ceiling.

"Those clouded eyes."

"Clouded eyes? I'm not sure I noticed that. But I will say he's an angry fellow."

"Big guy."

Tom laughs. "Yes, he's certainly been well fed."

"So you can see why I get frightened when I interview him?"

"Oh yes. Yes." I don't know whether Tom hears me. He looks to be deep in thought. "But, Scott, you know, you have to make more of an effort to connect to this man. He's frightening, but if you can overcome your anxiety and just talk to him, the two of you might have something to say to each other."

"Talk about what?"

"Anything. Sports, the weather, TV. If you can make a connection with him, you might find him less intimidating."

I run through some excuses that all together mean: I've tried, it's your turn. I'm not lazy, just impatient. I want Mr. Anastasi to improve when I say so. If he's not better by now, we'll have to wait until he's willing to cooperate with us.

"I don't question the effort you've made up to now," says Tom. "I think, though, that it's time to try something else."

As we talk, patients come up to us to pull at our sleeves. Once they have our attention, they let go and ask questions about their treatment: When do I get to go down to the day hospital? I want cafeteria privileges. I need money to make a phone call. Somebody stole my shoes.

"Maybe if I had coffee with him in the morning."

"It's worth a try."

"Am I doing something wrong?" I am desperate to know. "Should I see him more often?"

"It's not a question of seeing him more frequently. No. No, you're doing your job. What I'm saying is that Mr. Anastasi makes you anxious and that you need to find a way to overcome that anxiety. As long as you remain scared of him, you won't be able to help him."

"So I'm not doing anything wrong?"

"I didn't mean to add to your anxiety. Just think about what I've said and see what you can come up with."

Tom stands up abruptly and heads for the locked door. Before he can reach for his large metal key, the M.H.A. guarding the door lets him out. Left behind in the sitting room, I see patients wandering in circles. Most of them wear clothing that has been outgrown. Except for Mr. Plummer, leaning against a wall by the nurses' station. He's got on a camel hair sports coat, Italian shoes, and designer sunglasses. He looks Hollywood.

When he sees me staring at him from across the room, he crooks his index finger and signals me to come over.

"I want to talk to you," he says through a broad grin. "You've been avoiding me, and that isn't nice."

FOLLOWING
MR. PLUMMER

Mr. Plummer strides into his bedroom, and I follow him. He sits down on his well-made bed in the gray light. The bedroom could be an army barracks. It contains lockers and sleeps about a dozen people. Except for narrow rectangular apertures, the windows are sealed shut. The pale blue walls are bare. The room is spotless. Through the opened door, we can hear the TV in the adjacent dayroom loudly displaying *The $25,000 Pyramid*, a game show. I sit down on a bed facing Mr. Plummer. We look at one another awhile in silence. We are alone.

"I put in a three-day paper," he says. His voice is flat and emptied of feeling. He sounds like a phone recording of the time: At the tone, the time will be 2:52 and 40 seconds. "Three days and I am free to conduct my research."

A patient submits a three-day paper to indicate that he intends to leave the hospital within three days. Unless the paper is withdrawn, or the patient is ordered to be committed by a judge (on the basis of a doctor's recommendation), he must be released when the time is up. Following an initial observation period when they are first admitted to the hospital, patients are either released, committed against their will indefinitely, or admitted as *conditional voluntary* (CV) patients. CV patients agree to stay in the hospital and receive treatment; they may also put in a three-day paper at any time.

Committed individuals are viewed by the court as suicidal, homicidal, or unable to take care of themselves due to a major mental illness. Committed patients lose many rights. For example, they are no longer free to leave their assigned locked unit or the hospital grounds, unless they have attained a certain level of so-called privileges (for example, a day pass). They cannot make many crucial decisions about their private lives without the approval of their doctor.

A legal guardian may also be appointed for the patient by the court if his doctor feels that he cannot cooperate with necessary treatment (for example, taking medication). The guardian may be a family member, but if family is opposed, or wants to be left alone, a volunteer (often a member of the clergy and not usually known by the patient) is chosen by the presiding judge. The guardian also decides about participation in ECT (electroconvulsive therapy, used in the treatment of life-threatening depression when all other interventions have failed), if it is recommended.

During a commitment hearing, a judge comes to the hospital to hear evidence in support of hospitalizing an individual against his will. He meets the patient. Although commitment may be in a patient's long term best interests, the procedure can be time-consuming, unsavory, and initially counterproductive; for these reasons, the administration has urged us to get patients to sign themselves in voluntarily when they are seen to be in need of long-term in-patient care.

"Why do you want to leave the hospital?"

Mr. Plummer crosses his legs at the knees and strokes his chin in meditative fashion.

"I need to pick up several suits at the cleaners."

"Maybe someone in your family can do that for you."

"Don't be ridiculous."

He smirks. Typically, Mr. Plummer maintains stiff posture during a conversation. Except for his face. He uses his face to convey many feelings. He blinks, winces, smirks, and purses his lips. There is something infinitely sad about a man who chooses to censor and distort the expression of his inner life. When I look at Mr. Plummer, I feel as if I am looking at a child who is lost in a strange part of the city but is afraid to admit it.

"Please don't be absurd. Besides, the clothing isn't the nom de plume. I have lectures to prepare and research to complete. It's impossible for me to work here."

Since he returned from his escape, Mr. Plummer has insisted that he is "a world-famous specialist in pediatric medical surgery." He denies that he is the same man who was first brought in two weeks ago. He says it's a case of mistaken identity. And for several hours after his second admission, we weren't sure if he was the same man. I was able to identify him only by looking at his smooth hands, long fingers, and polished nails. His hands are beautiful; they could belong to a surgeon. But for the attention he pays to his hands, the new Mr. Plummer doesn't resemble the man who was brought in on a stretcher and shot up with Haldol against his will.

When he talks, it's clear that he's trying to sound like a man of science. He uses technical, abstract, and foreign words in an effort to describe simple feelings.

"How are you feeling this morning?"

"Prepped for neuropsychiatric surgery. The child must be saved."

When we are alone, the world becomes strange and distant. Mr. Plummer tells me stories that make sense only to the two of us. It's as if we're among the earth's last survivors. He sounds like a man who is tired of living. And yet, for all the emptiness he embodies, I feel soothed and fascinated by him. I love his fearlessness. I love the way he ignores his strangeness. I love his lack of anxiety. If he is Don Quixote tilting at windmills, then I am Sancho Panza.

"Have you tried to work here?"

"Quite obviously, atmospheric and neo-barometric pressures create implacable circumstances. I am due in Washington to provide a lecture series on pediatric medicine."

"If you could work here, what would you do?"

"The psychopharmacological approach to galvanic learning happens to be one I share. I would certainly want to avoid any redundancy over the medical model."

"Where will you go if you leave the hospital?"

"That's not your concern."

"Well, it is my concern," I insist. "You were brought back in here when the police found you wandering in the park. Neither of your parents will let you stay with them. You don't have any money. How can you say it's not my concern where you go? If you want to leave the hospital, let's at least figure out a plan."

When Mr. Plummer doesn't want to listen to me, he shuts his eyes, purses his lips, and becomes mute. We sit in silence for awhile. When he is ready to forgive me, he raises his eyelids, blinks rapidly, and moves his lips as if he is about to utter a sound. Nothing comes out. He is empty.

"Mr. Plummer? What's going on?"

"There's snow on the roof, but none in the basement."

"I don't understand."

"The lectures I am preparing require minimum research which I cannot delay. I must return to the pediatric unit in Bethesda and begin the surgery rotation."

Against my better judgment, I decide to use subterfuge to try to get Mr. Plummer to withdraw his three-day paper and instead sign himself in on CV status. I feel guilty and horrible about my trickery, but justify it by saying to myself that he's better off in Comm. Mental rather than roaming the streets. Also, it's what Tom wants, and what he wants, I want too.

"Perhaps you can study patients in the hospital. You could observe their behavior. Are you familiar with participant-observer studies?"

He nods his head yes.

"Well, why not conduct a participant-observer study here?"

"How?"

"You know, gather data as an in-patient. What happens to someone after they've been admitted to a hospital? Wouldn't it be interesting to look at your scientific concerns from the patient's perspective?"

"In other words, conduct my research as a patient?"

"Exactly."

"As a scientific participant?"

"As a participant-observer."

He strokes his chin, and turns his head in profile. He is struggling to maintain his dignity. I am ashamed of myself for not being straightforward. I owe him an honest relationship.

"I would need tools," he says after we spend several uncomfortable minutes in silence.

"What?"

"A notebook and some ballpoint pens."

"I can get them for you."

"And when my research is completed, I would like to present my findings to the staff here. Would that be possible? Could you arrange an appropriate forum for a lecture?"

"I think so."

When he finally signs the CV form (and withdraws the three-day paper), I feel like Lou Costello after he's sold a vacuum cleaner to some poor woman who doesn't need one. Mr. Plummer doesn't look much better. Does he understand what he's signed? If not, why did I encourage him to sign it? It is a harsh world if lying to a patient in order to get him to stay in the hospital looks like a better alternative to telling him the truth and letting him go free.

When we began talking, his posture was regal. Now he is hunched over like an old man on a long Sunday. He is preparing to play the role of a patient. No wonder he preferred pediatric surgery.

As the weeks go by, I learn about this man's history. He is thirty-two years old, the youngest child of parents who divorced when he left for college. There is an older sister who is a registered nurse. His mother is a fearful alcoholic who teaches physics in a public high school. His father is a tall, flashy dresser and fast-talker who still entertains fantasies of becoming a millionaire. He manages a small local nightclub on a part-time basis. The family is physically healthy. There is no history of mental illness. They are originally from Chicago.

When he was a high school student, Mr. Plummer excelled at long-distance running and academics. He worked extremely hard, applied to Bowdoin College, and was accepted with financial aid. He became an average college student. As was the case in junior high and high school, he had no friends at college, although he did have a girlfriend with whom he went out for over a year.

Until his junior year, no one paid much attention to him. Then he dropped acid a few times. After his drug experiences, he twice saw a psychologist at the health center. He complained of feeling lonely and isolated. Specifically, he felt that he was mistreated by students and faculty because he is black. He thought people were belittling him behind his back. He became active in the black student union and led a drive to petition the college to admit more black students.

After graduation, he returned to Boston to work as a writer at an advertising agency. No one knows why, but one day he stopped coming to work. He lost his job. He gave up his apartment, moved back in with his father, and began to argue about everything with both parents. Once he fought with his father physically.

Soon after, his college girlfriend jilted him because he started to "act weird." One night, when they were in bed, he stood over her and ordered her not to move until he said it was OK. While she cowered below, he posed like a statue. She waited a couple of hours, then ran out of the house.

He refused to leave his room. He became mute. He slept all day and stayed up all night. He talked loudly to himself. He began to hear great spiritual voices. He wrote biblical verses on the walls. He claimed that he was a prophet who could predict the future, read people's minds, and communicate telepathically.

Gradually, he began to suspect that others might be jealous

of him. He imagined that people wanted to rob him of his magical powers. He decided to try to win converts to his vague system of vague beliefs. One summer afternoon he was arrested and brought in to Comm. Mental for terrifying commuters downtown with a long religious harangue. He threatened them verbally. He violently resisted arrest.

Since he signed in as a CV, Mr. Plummer has assumed a leadership role among the patients in the locked unit. He stands beside the nurses' station most of the day and countermands doctors' medication orders. For example, if a patient is given a little cup of liquid medicine to take, Mr. Plummer takes the stuff from the patient's hand, sniffs it, and shakes his head no. Typically, the bewildered patient hands the cup back to a nurse.

He has also organized martial arts exercises in the dayroom. He invents the movements. He chants nonsense syllables while he makes arcs in the air.

Christina Signorelli, the nurse who customarily runs a morning exercise group for the patients, allows him to assist her because he enjoys the opportunity and is so good at it. The other nurses are not as generous as Christina. They tell Mr. Plummer to go away while they dispense medication to the other patients. They label his behavior "inappropriate." They feel that if he were on proper medication, he would be more cooperative.

They are especially annoyed when Mr. Plummer fakes his swallowing of the antipsychotic medicine he has been prescribed by my medical backup, Dr. Alice Duerler, a first-year psychiatry resident on day hospital one. He pops the pill in his mouth, tilts his head back, and appears to gulp. When a nurse asks him to open his mouth wide so she can look in, the pill is discovered beneath his quivering tongue.

Mr. Plummer also annoys staff when he refuses to leave the common shower room where he "prepares for pediatric surgery." He prepares by washing his hands repeatedly, holding them up to dry sterilized, and talking loudly to himself about "cleansing for pediatric obstetric surgery."

As the only "doctor" among the patients, he assumes a protective role with his more vulnerable comrades. For example, when he imagines that a patient is being threatened by another patient or a staff member, he intervenes. He cradles the victim and holds out his hand like a traffic cop. He breaks an important hospital rule with this intervention: no PC! PC stands for patient contact. Patients are strictly forbidden to touch one another. Despite staff's anger toward Mr. Plummer, many patients come to him for advice, or to be soothed. It is a wonder that they seek him out, since he is usually mute or incomprehensible.

"Are you Dr. Plummer's doctor?" I am asked by several patients.

"Yes."

"There's nothing wrong with him, you know. He's a good man. He's got religious powers. He listens to me."

The consensus among the nurses is that Mr. Plummer is "the craziest patient in the locked unit" and that "he should be forced to take medication." Many of them are becoming furious with me for my failure to push Mr. Plummer to take medication. When I tell them that I am opposed to medication for him because he doesn't want to take any and because I fear he will lose his creative spark, they tell me that I'm wrong.

"He's suffering, Scott," says Betty Anne. "And what are you doing to help him?"

In order to assess the nature of his madness, I decide to ask Mr. Plummer to undergo a full battery of psychological testing.

"Will you cooperate?" I ask him.

"Ocular," he says, and turns on his heel to drift back into the swirling mass of patients in the dayroom. His response is typical. What does he mean by "ocular"? That we see eye to eye? Or that we agree with one another, as in aye, aye?

Judith Rosen, the other psychology intern in day hospital one, agrees to test him. She gives him a Bender-Gestalt, a WAIS-R (I.Q.) test, Draw-A-Person, the T-A-T (Thematic Apperception Test), and the Rorschach. The testing takes far longer than expected because Mr. Plummer's verbalizations are complex, convoluted, and in-depth. He can't answer simply. He refers to himself when self-reference isn't necessary. He is concrete

when he should be abstract and abstract when he should be concrete. He is extremely inventive, but fails to observe accurately.

Mr. Plummer's T-A-T protocol is most interesting. The
T-A-T consists of a series of somewhat ambiguous black-and-
white drawings or photographs on eight-inch-by-eleven-inch
cards. The first card shows a little boy looking at a violin while
resting his chin on the palms of his hands. Another card shows
a farm scene: a man plows a field, a woman holds books in the
foreground, another woman on the side of the field appears to
be pregnant. A third card shows a man looking down, hat in
hand, while an older woman to his side looks out a window.
The instructions typically given for the T-A-T are: "Tell a story
about this picture. Your story must have a beginning, a middle,
and an end."

Judith is fascinated by Mr. Plummer's stories. They enter-
tain her. He builds suspense and provides surprise endings. His
language is lyrical.

"What's amazing," says Judith, "is how good the stories
are, especially in light of his general disorganization. If I only
looked at his Rorschach and his WAIS-R, I'd think he was probably a schizophrenic with borderline intelligence. But when I
look at the T-A-T, he looks super-bright and pretty well put
together. His stories are just incredible. I think they're good
enough to be published."

It would be a lot easier on us if Mr. Plummer behaved in a
consistent fashion. We would know what to expect of him. We
would know how to behave toward him. But someone suffering
from isolation, uncertainty, and auditory hallucinations is still a
human being with diverse, surprising qualities.

The psychological tests confirm that Mr. Plummer is psychotic. Probable diagnosis is schizophrenia (paranoid type) or
schizoaffective illness. A major difference between these two
diagnoses is that schizoaffective people seem to have greater
awareness of their feelings, and a greater capacity to use them
in their efforts to relate to others.

The factors that led to Judith's diagnostic impression are
specific and practical. Mr. Plummer cannot differentiate be-

tween himself and his surroundings. He has no consistent internal view of himself. He cannot establish boundaries with others. He has sad, delusional thoughts. He imagines his body crumbling, afire, divided, and exposed to instruments of torture. He hears voices that tell him that he is worthless and disgusting.

Going over the test results saddens me. Who is this man? How did his talents dissipate? I wonder what his parents imagined when they sent him off to college. Was he the great hope of the family? What dreams did they lose when he began to go mad?

Mr. Plummer tries to keep their dreams alive by acting out the pretense of being a physician. Once he was their star; now they'll be grateful if he can stay out of the mental hospital.

As the weeks go by, Mr. Plummer gets worse. His new camel hair sports coat becomes wrinkled and stained. He can't stop blinking when he talks. He has acquired an accent so that he now sounds like a brilliant African exchange student at a prestigious university. He speaks haltingly, but with precision. No matter what anyone says to him, he nods his head sagely, smiles condescendingly, and says, "yes, yes." The implication is that he and the speaker share a secret understanding.

"Mr. Plummer, we think you should take your medication."

"Yes, yes." He laughs dryly. His laughter sounds like that of a ventriloquist communicating through a dummy propped on his lap. Although he does not seem aware of being tense, Mr. Plummer's discomfort is evident in his empty expression. "Yes, yes."

When we meet, he is virtually mute. For a while, I cut down our time together. Then I try to engage him in a nonverbal activity. We play chess.

Mr. Plummer plays an excellent game in the midst of his psychotic storm. His one problem is a tendency to activate his most powerful pieces too early. Instead of relying upon pawns, knights, and bishops, he moves his queen and castles. He seeks a swift checkmate. In his haste to defeat the enemy, he leaves himself vulnerable to attack.

One day Mr. Plummer asks me if we can go off the locked unit together. He wants me to take him into the hospital courtyard.

"Why?"

"I remember a time when Jews were not afraid to call themselves Negroes," he answers.

I don't understand the meaning of this symbolic communication. Is he asking me to be more empathic? Perhaps he wants me to ask fewer questions and instead show more compassion. Perhaps he is merging with me. Perhaps he thinks we are parts of the same entity. Fascinated by his behavior, I agree to follow him where he wants to go.

I go to the nurses' station and sign him out. An M.H.A. unlocks the door of the unit, then swiftly locks it behind us. He winks at me through the small, eye-level observation window. Mr. Plummer and I ride the elevator down to the basement in silence.

We get out and walk the few steps to the courtyard. I unlock the door and follow Mr. Plummer in. I lock the door behind us. We have never been here before.

The courtyard is surrounded by five stories of brick and sealed windows. It looks as if we are in a vacant lot. Locust trees, weeds, and shrubs grow haphazardly. The ground is covered with leaves, tall grass, and candy wrappers. Because we are in a vacuum, the wind gusts powerfully. Dust gets in my eyes and irritates them.

I follow Mr. Plummer as he walks through the tall, wild grass. He moves rapidly, and I hop beside him in an effort to keep up. The wind howls, blowing refuse around us in colorful swirls. He looks straight ahead. He blinks and crosses his arms. Then, without looking at me, he begins to speak. He has a story to tell, and this is where he wants to tell it. As he talks, I imagine that he is King Lear and I am the fool.

"I remember when you went to Hebrew school. It was around the time when my son celebrated his bar mitzvah. Yes,

I remember it well. After his bar mitzvah, I was sent to boot camp in North Korea. We had to fight as well as perform surgery. The work was extremely difficult. We had to fight even though it was very cold. The nights were freezing. Many men came down with frostbite. Their toes and fingers snapped off. But I had to go on with my duties.

"When boot camp ended, I served in a mobile medical unit. I was with my best friend, a man named Cohen. Once, on patrol, I saw a burning building that had been bombed by the North Koreans. I heard screams inside it. I rushed in and saw a young girl and two old ladies. I tried to rescue them, but the building started to collapse. Beams crashed all around me. I had the girl in my arms, but I didn't see how we could escape.

"But then Cohen rescued me. He crashed through the entrance with his huge bazooka. He had a big, big bazooka. He carried me out. He saved my life."

He stops his passionate speech and looks around blankly. He is out of breath. Reciting his tale has drained him. Never before has he shown me so much vitality. It's a shame that the story is delusional. He's too young to have served in Korea. He has no son. He is not Jewish.

But if his story is fictional, psychologically it is true. He feels like a soldier in this hospital; his room resembles a barracks. He feels close to Jews; his doctor is a Jew. He feels exhausted as if by battle. He feels engulfed as if by flames. He cannot take care of himself. He wants to share his burden. He wants to be saved before it's too late. He is frightened and miserable, but he is a courageous man. He risks his life to save others.

I decide to share some of my impressions with him.

"Your story reminds me of your situation here in the hospital. Because you are busy helping others, you end up feeling trapped and overwhelmed. You want someone to help you."

His response to my interpretation isn't encouraging.

"Excuse me," he says, and walks behind an enormous bush to pee. When he returns, he has a request for me.

"Say 'bip, bip, bip, woo, woo, woo.' "

"What?"

"Say 'bip, bip, bip, woo, woo, woo.' "

"Why? What does it mean?"

"Say it."

I always try to avoid making ambiguous remarks. But Mr. Plummer won't budge.

"Let's go upstairs now," I suggest.

"Not until you say 'bip, bip, bip, woo, woo, woo.' "

I avoid a confrontation. After all, what could happen if I do what he wants?"

"Bip, bip, bip," I whisper. I have a vision of my supervisors standing beside me with looks of condemnation on their faces.

"Woo, woo, woo."

The moment after I say the last "woo," Mr. Plummer raises his hands high up in the air, jerks his body forward, and performs the most spectacular and surprising cartwheel I have ever seen.

"I learned that command in boot camp," he says. He brushes dirt off his palms. "I'm ready to go upstairs now."

I unlock the door and follow him out.

IN THE LOCKED UNIT

AT HOME

I unlock the thick steel door. The key is three inches long. It weighs an ounce. Sonny, an M.H.A., motions for me to come forward. Then he locks us in. I follow my parent. I meant to write, "I follow my *patient.*" Why the confusion? What about Mr. Plummer makes me think of my father? Is it because he also appears to me to be aloof and strange? (My father is a German Jew who came to this country in August 1941 on the final Jewish children's transport permitted to leave that country. Along with an older brother who survived a slave labor camp in Riga, Latvia, and a few first cousins who emigrated to Israel and the United States in the late 1930s, he is the last remnant of a large family whose roots in southern Germany, I am told, reach back to the fourteenth century). Is it because I follow in my father's footsteps? (He is also a clinical psychologist.) Is it because my father's playful mien often masks sad feelings? (He seems at times to live in a haunted house he can't get away from. The ghosts are very attached to me. I mean *him*. I meant to write *him*.)

Countertransference describes the experience in which the psychotherapist's feelings about a loved one are transferred onto a patient. Is this what is happening to me? How does this complicate my treatment of Mr. Plummer?

Although he moves slowly, I am always a few steps behind him. Mr. Plummer is at home in the locked in-patient unit, but I'm not. He moves proudly and authoritatively. He makes me think of Sydney Carton in *The Tale of Two Cities,* who sacrificed himself for Charles Darnay, whose life he judged to be more important. He feels worthless and dissolute; ironically, only through the sacrifice of death does his life achieve its true meaning. Is this a clue to understanding Mr. Plummer? Or is it a clue to understanding my father? My confusion helps to explain why supervision and psychotherapy for us interns is so crucial during the internship (and afterward). I must continue to develop awareness of where my feelings end, where the patient's begin, and where they meet to achieve new meaning.

As we inch through the dayroom, numerous patients interrupt their activities to greet Mr. Plummer with shy, fragile, tentative half-waves. They don't know how he will react to a simple act of kindness. Rashid, an M.H.A. who is playing Ping-Pong with Frank, a young black man in pajamas and green foam slippers, breaks his serve to nod hello. His opponent claims the point and we move past them, as they argue, toward the nurses' station. Mr. Plummer does not acknowledge anyone's presence. He looks straight ahead. He moves stiffly, a fast clip, a militaristic pace. Where is he heading with such great speed and intensity?

When we reach the wall opposite the entrance to the unit, Mr. Plummer stops abruptly, does an about-face, and surveys the dayroom. He crosses his arms. He stands a few inches from the wall. He begins to stroke his chin. He appears to start whispering. I lean closer in order to hear him better, only to discover that he is moving his lips without saying a word. He stares straight ahead. I follow his gaze.

The air is thick with clouds of cigarette smoke. I hear a Tom and Jerry cartoon on the television in the other dayroom down the corridor; it sounds as if either the mouse or the cat is getting clobbered again. No one in the room reacts visibly to the chaos. They are preoccupied. What might they be thinking about? The teenage daughter of a man who suffers from psychosis described her father to me: "He talks to himself about sad things that happened a long time ago and only mean something to him." Perhaps this description applies to the people I see in this room.

The floor is tiled with linoleum that is stained indelibly. A Ping-Pong table dominates the center of the room. A game between Rashid and Frank has resumed: ping! pong! ping! pong! Surrounding the two players are two lumpy chairs upholstered in brown plastic and a long, busted couch with a wooden frame. The furniture may have been donated by friends of the hospital. It resembles the junk I have seen dumped curbside on the first days of April. No one needs it anymore.

Naturally, the patients mirror the condition surrounding them. Most act like they don't care about themselves. I smell urine, feces, and sweat from their unwashed bodies. Solitary action is characteristic. Ritually, they rock back and forth in the chairs, pace the floor narrowly, gesticulate with their hands, gesture with their bodies, or talk to voices. The voices they hear are typically evil and disembodied. They say morbid, insulting, disgusting, and horrifying words that relentlessly terrify, humiliate, and sadden the helpless listeners. A few patients sit in stony silence, looking as if they are praying for an end to their misery. One man, a small, balding figure with an unshaven face and caved-in shoulders, says suddenly: "Well. Marx and Freud. That's academic. It was sucking doggies' dicks, you know." Then he giggles, wipes his mouth with the back of a chapped hand, and rocks himself back into silence. He wears a silly grin.

If any of this makes an impression on Mr. Plummer, he doesn't show it. He stands there and takes it all in. He acts like the participant-observer I conned him into playing. He murmurs knowledgeably, nods his head up and down, and then, without a word, turns and walks down the short corridor that leads to the other dayroom. We pass by the examining room, the nurses' station, the showers, and the kitchen. We enter the dayroom where the TV is playing and stand here for a while. Then we enter Mr. Plummer's room. He kicks off his shoes and lies down on his bed. With his eyes closed, his arms stiffened by his sides, and his posture rigid and painfully correct, he looks like a corpse in an open casket.

I stand over him. His closed eyelids begin to flutter rapidly. His face looks like a mask hammered into copper. I wish he would display feelings or thoughts easily acceptable to me. Instead, he embodies disintegration. And as I stand beside his still form, I feel overwhelmed by just a little bit of the immense loneliness he has to live with all the time. How can I help him if proximity only makes me want to create distance?

Peggy Eagleton, the clinical psychologist who supervises my work with Mr. Plummer, makes a helpful suggestion: "Sit with him in silence, if necessary, but sit with him. He knows you're there. I once had a catatonic patient whom I met with regularly. I sat beside her on the floor. When she improved, she thanked me for that time when I gave to her without being acknowledged."

Peggy then tells me about Hermann Merart, a late psychoanalyst whose work at Comm. Mental I will continue to hear about frequently during the year. Merart's thoughts on the mentally ill are the cornerstone of teaching at Comm. Mental. He loved his patients, and accorded them the respect one gives to the suffering. He rarely used jargon. He preferred humor and simplicity. From Prentiss Cliff to senior psychiatry residents, Merart is revered like a saint. I am to hear plenty of anecdotes about him. The one I remember best is a story about how Merart kept a hot plate and frying pan in his office. He loved fried eggs. A rumor exists that he cooked eggs occasionally for some of his patients. It would have been a simple way to feed their psychological hunger.

"And get into therapy," counsels Peggy. "Your anxieties about your own feelings are getting in the way of your ability to listen to your patients. An internship is very stressful. I know, I started therapy during my internship and now, eight years later, I'm still seeing the same therapist."

She tells me about a program at Beth Israel hospital that provides psychotherapy to psychology interns during their internship year. Clinical psychologists who practice in Boston and Cambridge offer their services at greatly reduced rates to participants in the program.

"You seem to be extremely anxious about yourself. We've all noticed it. And we're concerned about you. Has Edith spoken to you about it?"

Each of the psychology interns is assigned a chief supervisor at the start of the year. Edith Katz is my chief supervisor. I meet with her once a week to discuss all aspects of the internship. Edith is a petite former Oklahoman who attended Barnard College during the Vietnam era. She has long black hair, worn in the style of the late 1960s, and is rather partial to long peasant skirts and cowboy boots. She never critiques my work directly. I often have a very hard time figuring out what she is trying to tell me. She is indirect. She has a fine, throaty laugh and for reasons I haven't quite figured out reminds me of Janis Joplin. She also makes me think of a huge folk singer in Harvard Square whose songs all sound the same, with smug lyrics like: "And where have all the children gone? And the plants, and animals, and stuff? It's bombs that frighten life away, haven't we had enough? (Repeat.)"

"Yes."

"I think it's affecting your work."

Actually, just about all of the staff in the psychology department has spoken to me about my anxiety and how they guess they feel it's affecting my work: Robin Archer, Robert Hamilton, Edith Katz, and now Peggy. In the psychiatry department, Tom Downes and Eleanor Stonehill, the chief psychiatry resident of day hospital one, have also talked to me about my evident difficulties. Eleanor has observed, for example, that I have a tendency to intellectualize or to make people laugh as a way of creating emotional distance. In response to this observation, I spoke haughtily about the complicated issues that are part of being the son of a psychologist. I told her that my girlfriend and I had just broken up after going out for the past four years. I tried to make her laugh, and succeeded.

Predictably, I respond with great defensiveness to what I experience as charges against my character. Peggy looks genuinely sad as she listens passively to my brittle anger, denial, and distortion.

When I finish ranting, she shrugs her diminutive shoulders. "It's up to you."

My sessions with Mr. Plummer continue in the locked in-patient unit for weeks without any abatement of his suffering. With the help of Carol Silber, the social worker assigned to his case, I gather information about his history. The facts are psychiatrically sparse and impersonal. For example, we learn that he was first hospitalized nine years ago. Since then he has been hospitalized eighteen different times for periods ranging from ten to sixty days. Diagnostic impression, using the classification of the *DSM-III-R,* has typically been: "295.92. Schizophrenia, undifferentiated, chronic." The diagnosis is a kiss of death because with that label staff often feels that the patient is beyond the reach of their love. They may not want to extend themselves to someone who won't get better anyhow.

Mr. Plummer's history also contains information about the antipsychotic medications he has been treated with: Haldol, Mellaril, Prolixin, Thorazine, Narvane. Mr. Plummer's reaction to these medications, according to the chart review, has sometimes been negative: weight loss, tardive dyskinesia, sexual impotence. There is no mention of a drug that has proven to be efficacious. No wonder Mr. Plummer is resistant to taking medication again, and no wonder he thinks of himself as a medical specialist. In a way, he is.

"I think we should conference the family," says Carol. "You're not making much progress with John, I mean, he isn't getting any better, and having information about the family should be of help. I've been meeting with mother and father. And they're definitely a big part of son's problem."

I agree at once, for several reasons. Carol's clinical perspective is different from mine. She doesn't use the pronouns "his" or "her" before "mother" and "father." She seems to capitalize these words in her mind: Family as Historical Entity. I want to see his life from a fresh perspective. I also need help. Working individually with Mr. Plummer frightens and drains me. I would like to feel supported. Finally, Carol suggests that we may have the opportunity to present the Plummer family to Alex Ellmann, one of the most popular and brilliant psychiatrists on staff here.

Alex Ellmann wowed the hospital recently at Grand Rounds. Grand Rounds is held every Wednesday afternoon. It provides a forum for some of the big-name psychiatrists in town. In an unpretentious way, Alex quoted the writings of Dostoevsky, D. H. Lawrence, and a number of modern poets in his talk. He spoke with spontaneity, ease, and humor. He feels that literature can tell us as much as a great many psychoanalytic texts. He appreciates the range of possibilities that exist for people.

Carol and I will need to persuade the Plummer family to allow themselves to be the focus of a conference. We must also convince Alex Ellmann that meeting with them is worth his time. He is said to be extremely busy, a real star on the psychiatric hospital lecture circuit.

Carol and I hold a mini-summit with the Plummer family in my office on the day hospital. The atmosphere is a tight fit. Mother and father no longer speak to one another outside of meetings convened by their son's therapists. They can agree readily about only one thing: life at home would have been dandy if it had not been for their crazy son.

Of course, this isn't the case. Father sits with legs crossed tightly, hair thick with pomade, full of a girlish sort of mirth. He flirts with his son throughout the meeting. He doesn't listen to a word anyone says. He is restless, spidery, easily distracted. He refers everything back to himself. He reminds me of Richard Simmons, the host of the exercise program on TV. Mother looks much older than her ex-husband. She appears to be unsure of her importance. Son is mute.

As the meeting progresses, I think of Mr. Plummer as an artist in a high-wire act. He works without a net. Below him is misery and delusion. Mom holds one end of the rope, dad holds the other. We all must try at times to balance ourselves between our parents' perceptions of who we are, but in his case the struggle always leads to failure. The rope is taut: it is loose; it is taut; it is loose. He never manages to please them both. They feel that he failed them by becoming mentally ill; they had hoped, rather, that he would become a doctor. And he never manages to step off the rope and pursue his real desires elsewhere.

When Carol brings up the topic of a family conference, mother and father agree at once. Sure, why not? They are on an altogether different wavelength. When I bring up medication, their son, oddly, agrees to a trial of antipsychotics. He nods his head up and down. Is he trying to please mother and father? Does he know what he wants for himself? I am about to celebrate because of his choice, whatever the reason for the switch, but then father speaks up, and I realize suddenly that it's too early to claim victory.

"I don't want to denigrate your profession . . ." he says.

"Good!" I interject.

". . . but my son is not a guinea pig for experimental drugs."

"These drugs aren't experimental. They may help him to control his thoughts."

"Well, I don't want them to interfere with our jogging together. How can he play sports with poison in his brain?"

"But they're not poison."

"We want to help John," adds Carol.

"Well, I just don't agree with you. I'm sorry, but I don't."

Mr. Plummer shakes his head from side to side to indicate that he refuses again to take the medication. Carol and I are furious with father. Mother doesn't say a word. The meeting ends abruptly.

Mother clutches her square black pocketbook. She kisses

her son on the cheek. He towers over her. He has to bend down to meet her embrace. She leaves alone. Then father and son take the stairs down to the cafeteria in the cellar. I follow them and eavesdrop on their conversation over coffee.

Father: "What a pretty sweater you have on! You've got on your pretty sweater! How nice! How nice it looks!"

Son: (Smiles)

Father: "Now what's that smile about? Hmm? Such a pretty smile!"

Overhearing their conversation depresses me. How is help possible if so much has to change along with the individual? I go back upstairs feeling hopeless.

When I return to my office, there's a note under my door from Carol. Alex Ellmann has agreed to lead a conference with the Plummer family.

That night I return to my apartment in the North End. I drink three beers and eat a tuna sandwich I'd forgotten to take to work. Through the paper-thin walls, I hear the people in the apartment next door watching Johnny Carson. Twice since I moved here in June I've been awakened by their lovemaking in the early morning. I switch on the TV. An amazing coincidence: it's Richard Simmons and he's moving at a speed few maniacs ever achieve.

The family conference takes place, as usual, in the chapel. Over fifty staff, residents, interns, and nurses have gathered on an assemblage of metal folding chairs with gold cushions. Carol, Alex Ellmann, and the Plummer family sit in a semicircle on a small proscenium before us. I present a brief history of my work with Mr. Plummer, Carol gives a synopsis of her work with mother and father, and then Alex takes over.

There is usually a certain theatricality to a case presentation at conferences. Patients presented often feel humiliated by having to divulge intimate details about their lives before so many strangers. A current joke among our group of interns and residents is that a conference is deemed successful if the discussant can make the patient cry. Or to put it another way, "enable the patient to display some affect."

Alex is extremely sensitive, however, to the possible humiliation of the Plummer family. He behaves conspiratorially. Although I sit in the front row, for example, I have to lean forward to hear him. He is whispering. He only asks them questions that they may have already asked themselves in private. He doesn't exploit their weaknesses. He reacts with genuine awe and respect to their comments. If it is Them and Us, he makes it clear that he is one of Them.

The family is soothed by him. They speak openly about the choices they've made. They begin to treat each other with the respect Alex accords them. They listen to one another.

When the meeting ends, mother slips as she steps off the raised platform. Father breaks her fall by catching her at the elbow. They look as if they are about to leave on a lunch date. Son follows them out, zombielike, his face a total blank. Although I am no closer to understanding how I can be of help to him, Alex has enabled me to see the Plummer family without their disguises. He allowed them to be themselves.

At 2:30 A.M. I am awakened by a dream about Mr. Plummer. I stand beside the order book in the nurses' station of the locked in-patient unit. I have just written an order: Patient cured of current mental illness. (signed) DR. Scott Haas. "DR." was written in bold, capital letters. Do I want to be DR. Alex Ellmann? Do I want to be my father, the real DR. Haas? Do I want to get a good night's sleep? I feel powerful, but sick to my stomach, and a total fake. How can I help anyone if I don't know what my true feelings are about myself?

By the end of the week, Mr. Plummer is forbidden by Gertrude, the head nurse of the in-patient unit, to lead any more exercise groups.

"It's inappropriate," she says. I hate that word. It has come to mean any behavior the staff doesn't like. For example, it is "inappropriate" for patients to touch one another ("NO PC!"—

"no patient contact"), to disobey doctor's orders, to talk back to staff, or to question beyond a superficial level the rules of the in-patient unit. "John's a patient here, not one of the staff."

"Well, I don't see what's wrong with his leading a few exercises in the morning."

"You don't see what's wrong with it." She turns her back and starts to walk away. "Well, maybe you ought to think more about how you're going to get him to take medication and less about whether or not he should be jumping around all morning in front of the other patients."

At this point, I want Mr. Plummer to take medication if for no other reason than to regain respect and cooperation I've lost from staff. With the head nurse against me, I won't get much accomplished on the unit. Silently, she will place obstacles in my path. For example, at a time when I have scheduled to meet with a patient, she will arrange for that person to be out on a group walk or taking a shower. Or when I need privacy to conduct an interview, she will make certain that none is available. More subtly, she and the other nurses will follow through on my orders only halfheartedly.

Within days of my exchange with Gertrude, Mr. Plummer's condition deteriorates rapidly. He wears cotton pajamas and a thin, blue-striped bathrobe all day. He makes a turban out of a scarf on his head. He walks from spot to spot in the dayrooms, moves his hands as if performing prestidigitation, and chants an incantation.

One morning, I am approached by Kerry, an individual in her early twenties with borderline intellect, who also carries a diagnosis of schizophrenia. She is sort of the mascot of the in-patient unit, and the favorite of Betty Anne, the assistant head nurse. And so although we have not been introduced to one another, Kerry feels comfortable enough to approach me. It's as if we have heard about each other through a mutual friend.

"Hey! Hey, Scott!" She tugs at the shirtsleeve above my elbow. We stand in the short corridor between the dayrooms. Doctors race by, patients shuffle along. It is hard to hear her above the din and commotion, but there's no place else to talk except for her bedroom and that's out of the question. "I gotta talk to you."

We stand off to the side and pretend that no one can hear us. Kerry cups her hands to my ear and whispers, "It's about John. He's acting real crazy, Scott. I'm worried about him."

"I know." I nod my head up and down. "You're right."

"He won't talk to nobody."

"I know."

"So you gotta do something."

"What?"

She backs off with an astonished face.

"You're the doctor!" She points at me as if it's an accusation. "How should I know?"

I decide to ask Tom to conference Mr. Plummer. Each Thursday morning a patient is interviewed by the super-chief of one of the day hospitals before the in-patient staff. We get together on a bunch of beat-up chairs in a small room in a corner of the building. After I present a history, noteworthy mostly for my omissions, disorganization, and tension, Tom pointedly asks for more basic info that I cannot provide. What is happening to me? Why can't I buckle down and do the work?

The demands made on me are simple and clear enough. A history typically follows a format: patient's presenting complaint: history of presenting complaint; medical history; psychiatric history; educational and vocational history; family history; treatment plans; current course of treatment; questions for the discussant. My presentation lacks many details. Perhaps like the angry head nurse, I act my anger out in terms of what isn't said, and in terms of what I leave out. What am I so angry about? I don't know.

Following Tom's criticism of my poor presentation, Rashid leads Mr. Plummer in like a fine race horse. He acts like a specimen rather than a man. He knows he is being observed closely for any flaws, and he works hard to create a barrier that isn't easily penetrable in order to hide them. Tom stands up and shows him to a seat. He and Mr. Plummer sit a few feet away from the general assembly. Tom is bent forward, knees crossed, his arms squeezed around his chest and shoulders. His right hand holds his left elbow. His left hand is pressed flat against his face. He reminds me of Jack Benny talking to Rochester. The boss speaks to the employee. Neither man is straightforward. They both play roles that sever connections.

The conferences always begin with silence. The discussant stares at the patient. The patient tries to show some poise. With a mute person like Mr. Plummer, we're likely to remain in silence for the entire ninety minutes. Finally, Tom speaks up.

"I guess you know all of the people in this room. Is there anyone here you don't know?"

Silence. No movement at all.

"How are you feeling, Mr. Plummer? I guess I'm asking because we're all very concerned about you."

"I feel fine. And I'm grateful for the opportunity to present some of my research, doctor, in this professional setting before colleagues."

"Ah. Yes?"

"In my professional experience, the neuropediatric condition requires some, ahh, amelioration through surgical procedures. But naturally the psychopharmacological route is one that is also taken. You may open your notebooks at this time and begin to take notes. That will not disturb me."

"Mr. Plummer, I'm afraid I don't understand. I'm afraid you don't understand either."

"I would like to continue my lecture. Please save your questions for the end."

John Kantrowitz, one of the psychiatry residents, begins to giggle helplessly. He sets off a wave of giggling. Nurses and doctors cover their mouths with appointment books and whatever else is handy. What's funny about a man who is out of control? Even Tom looks like he is about to laugh aloud.

There is something charming, sweet, and gentle about Mr. Plummer. He reminds me of a child who has come to show his parents some trifle he believes to be the ultimate achievement and sure to please them. Maybe what's funny is that when he opens his hands to reveal the surprise, nothing is there. He has delighted them with invisibility.

"Please continue," says Tom.

Mr. Plummer talks about surgery, endocrine levels, hormonal imbalances, and phenothiazines. Nothing he says invites a response. We don't understand him. And, ironically, the more he talks, the more distant we become from him. I try to imagine how it would be if talking to others made me feel more alone in the world, rather than closer, rather than loved.

"And of course there are the neuroleptics," he says. He wears the same blank expression. "Thorazine, Haldol, Stellazine, and Octane."

"Octane?"

"A new class of drugs."

Finally, Mr. Plummer is escorted out. The last phase of the conference begins. We discuss the patient in his absence. Tom smiles gently, shakes his head, and murmurs, "Octane. Wow." Kantrowitz slaps his thighs and laughs loudly. "Octane!" he shouts. We all start to laugh a little bit, relieved that the patient isn't with us anymore. His madness is scary. It has to stop. The nurses are especially discomfiting. They have little clinical supervision. This isn't a learning experience for them like a residency or internship; it's a job.

"Well, Scott, I think we have to start thinking about guardianship," says Tom. "Mr. Plummer is clearly unable to look out for his best interests. I don't think we'll have much trouble having a guardian appointed for him. And then we can get him started on some meds."

I show opposition to the plan due, again, to my ambivalence about placing him on medication. The head nurse leads a chorus of sighs. Tom stands firm.

"Just do it. Eleanor will show you how to do the paperwork for a guardianship. It's not difficult. But everything needs to be carefully documented before we go before a judge."

I slam the door on my way out, feeling stupid and ashamed. I still cling to old-fashioned ideas about schizophrenia, which view the disorder as amenable to psychodynamic psychotherapy.

"Sure, sure," Peggy says later on, "but medication can't be excluded from the treatment plan. It has an important role in Mr. Plummer's therapy. Think of it as part of the psychotherapy. And think of his pain."

And so I go about arranging for Mr. Plummer's guardianship. First, we arrange to have him committed. Then, Eleanor helps me to document the course of his stay at the hospital. It has not been beneficial. Because of his refusal to take medication or to attend groups, Mr. Plummer has deteriorated considerably. We make a case to present before the judge.

There is something insidious about taking away a man's freedom because he uses it to make decisions I don't agree with. What an awesome responsibility it is for the doctor to decide that he knows best! But, in fact, it's sometimes true that people don't know how to choose the right sort of assistance. (I guess.) Coming from a family, however, where my father's parents and sister had their freedom taken away leads me to identify with people who are powerless. (They were murdered because they were Jews.) Do I identify with this patient too much? Does my personal history really have anything to do with Mr. Plummer's life and his needs? Is this another experience of countertransference?

It doesn't matter much, because if I don't do what I'm told, Tom will be furious. So I sign the right documents and Mr. Plummer is on his way toward having a guardian appointed who will make decisions on his behalf. I feel like a collaborator with the enemy.

A month later, Eleanor, Tom, and I go before a judge who sits in a small room off the lobby. He visits Comm. Mental now and then to preside over guardianship hearings. The patient has a court-appointed attorney present. Everyone, except for Mr. Plummer, is very chummy. *We're not like him* seems to be the hidden message. *We're doing the right thing.* We show the judge our documents. He puts on a pair of gold-rimmed bifocals, reads through some papers, shuffles others in an important, harried way. The patient is asked to speak, but he remains mute. He's asked a few questions. He speaks up. His answers indicate clearly that he is very disoriented. And he certainly looks crazy. He keeps making all sorts of very peculiar movements with his facial musculature. He smiles, winces, and then gestures with his hands. It's all over in less than fifteen minutes. The judge appoints the guardian.

Our therapy session immediately following the guardianship focuses primarily on Mr. Plummer's need to be what is termed "med. compliant," meaning that he will comply with doctor's orders to take medication. After I feel that the message has gotten across to him, we walk together to the nurses' station. A nurse offers him a cup of water and two pills. One pill is Haldol, an antipsychotic medication; the other is Cogentin, a medication that helps to control the side effects of the Haldol. Mr. Plummer looks at them and then walks away. I tag along. He comes to a full stop in the dayroom, where the TV is blaring. Its noise makes conversation almost impossible. You can't hear yourself think, which, I suppose, is the point.

"Mr. Plummer? Mr. Plummer, I have to tell you that unless you agree to take the medication voluntarily, they're going to give it to you I.M., through injections. It's up to you. You have three days to decide."

I feel like crying. I imagine that I am telling my father that he's being deported. Boy, am I ever confused! Mr. Plummer walks away. He doesn't look at me. Three days later he takes the pills.

In the weeks following his compliance, Mr. Plummer initially shows more willingness to talk to staff. On occasion, he smiles when something funny happens or is said, rather than at a private experience he can't share readily with anyone else. He displays more of a so-called appropriate range of affect, meaning that he doesn't look strictly empty or sad. As a reward for his efforts, in response to these changes, the treatment plan is altered. He is now brought down to the day hospital for a few hours each morning. Here he can engage in groups and activities that require a higher level of ego functioning.

Despite the overall improvement, however, he is still psychotic. For example, when I ask him how he feels about the day hospital, he says, "It's unsafe waters. Territoriality and tantamountality."

"Do you mean you don't feel safe on the day hospital?"

His response: "In many ways I consider myself the expectorant of an admiral, the Archbishop of Canterbury. And if you say the waters are safe, well, then it's no certainty."

Schizophrenic language is elegant. It makes a metaphor out of reality. Is it only a sign that the person is suffering? Or is Mr. Plummer also tuned in to another, more poetic frequency? He can't forget the past. He can't tell the difference between his dreams and reality. He is frightened and alone. But despite the visionary aspects of his personality, he just can't see what Ralph Ellison, writing in *Invisible Man*, termed "the recognition of possibility." Mr. Plummer can't imagine being other than mad or empty.

After three days, due to his inability to participate in any of the day hospital activities, I place him back on third-floor restrictions. He leaves the locked in-patient unit only to come to my office twice weekly for therapy. An excerpt from a recent session:

Therapist: I hear that you're having trouble staying on the third floor.

Patient: Solar energy.

T: Maybe I can arrange for you to have some hours out with staff supervision. You know, staff walks to the courtyard. How would that be?

P: I want a full discharge so that I can get an apartment, begin a new life, and apply to law school. Also, I want my medications, my medications less . . . less . . . what's the word?

T: Tapered?

P: Yes. I want my medications tapered.

T: What does the medication do for you?

P: It sedates me.

T: Well, it also makes you more organized and clear.

P: That's your opinion.

T: What do you think we want to give you medication for?

P: As part of an experiment for the drug companies.

T: I don't have any stock in drug companies. You're too suspicious. I think the medication makes you feel sad. And that's what you mean by a sedating effect.

P: That's nonsense you use to justify your job. The staff behaves one way in the day hospital, another way at home. That's not really how you feel about medication.

T: Look, I want to help you. Maybe that's difficult for you to accept.

P: No. It's just that I don't need the kind of help you have to offer.

T: What sort of help do you need?

P: I need to be discharged.

T: That's something we need to negotiate. I need, for example, to know more about how you're feeling.

P: Fine! I'm feeling fine!

By the time my internship ends on the last day of June, Mr. Plummer's condition is virtually unchanged. We sit in my office twice a week, frequently in silence; sometimes we play chess; when we talk, his speech is lyrical. Now he leaves the locked unit to be brought down to a few day-hospital activities, and for the occasional day pass. By the end of our time together, I have come to accept him for who he is, rather than who I would like him to be. I stop trying to change him or to make him better. I enjoy his company. I'm not frightened of him anymore. I look forward eagerly to his visits. Perhaps that's how treatment *begins,* by caring about a person whose suffering seems complete, whose shame about himself must be accepted before he can feel unashamed, by identifying truly with his predicament and not just those parts that seem the most familiar. In this way, he becomes my patient, and not my parent.

MR. ANASTASI/EDDIE

I start each morning at the hospital by having a coffee with Mr. Anastasi. We sit side by side on a couch in the locked unit. Its old foam cushions sink to the floor from our weight. Our elbows rest on our knees. We look as if we've both been bent in half and can't get up without a helping hand. Will we ever straighten out? Our hands cup Styrofoam containers of mud-colored coffee. Steam rises to our faces and clings there. The unit stirs to life after a restless night of new admissions and changes in shift. I hear screams of fear and inconsolable loneliness: sobbing, and then a woman whose voice sounds as if she is being strangled: "I want to die! I want to die! Get away from me! Leave me alone! LEAVE ME ALONE!" And then sobbing, again. But we collude and pretend to ignore what's going on around us. Mr. Anastasi behaves like a factory worker on break (which I suppose is true); and I act like a kid fresh out of college on a goofy sort of project for a psychology course (which I suppose is also true). We don't talk.

During the half hour that we are together, I find it hard to

keep my mouth shut. I think of graduate school in Detroit, where
Harvey Myers, one of the professors, made the point that it was
best for us to say as little as possible, preferably nothing, in
psychotherapy sessions. We had just started to see our first patients.

"You, must, uh, allow the, uh, patient to, uh, associate
freely without interfering. You are the, uh, blank, uh, slate, that
psychoanalytic theory refers to as the, uh, so-called transferen-
tial object. Or, uhh, the *tabula rasa.*" He pauses to puff on his
pipe; his lower lip bulges out; I think of the character Bleistein
in the semi-eponymous poem by T. S. Eliot; Harvey holds the
pipe by its bowl and says, "Unless you have something to say,
uh, why say anything?"

Harvey is a small man who still talks with a thick Brooklyn
accent, a remnant of the place where he grew up. He drives an
enormous pearl-gray Cadillac to work. He smokes a pipe steadily and always hesitates between words as he talks. He wears a
different new and beautiful suit to each of the weekly lectures.
He lights up with matchbooks from Detroit's poshest restaurants. The only other advice I remember that he gave me came
when I walked him out once to his car in the parking lot behind
the department. He unlocked and opened the door, turned to
me, and said, "Never live closer than 750 miles from your
mother and father." Then he got in, buckled up, and drove off.

As I sit with Mr. Anastasi, I begin to count silently;
one, one thousand, two, two thousand, three, three thousand,
four, four thousand, five, five thousand. . . .

Supervisors tend to guide my thoughts and actions. When
they're nowhere in sight, I picture them beside me. When I have
an original thought, I try to twist it until it conforms handily to
what I already know to be true. Perhaps it's fair to amend Harvey's
advice about one's mother and father to include supervisors.

Mr. Anastasi turns to me and grunts. I smile my very best
smile. Suddenly I'm in a staring contest. I try to mimic his
features. Then I figure, what the hell, this can't go on all morning, I've really got to say something, anything.

"How are you doing?"

"OK."

Thus, our longest exchange to date. I still have no idea what he's thinking. He just glares at me until I feel small. I fall back on textbook interview to tide me over. At this point, anything is better than silence. We have to keep moving along. Even if it means asking a few stupid questions.

"What's it like being here for you?"

"What makes you wanna know?"

"Curious."

"Uh huh."

He sips his coffee and returns to profile. I look at him for awhile. His effort and concentration go into holding the cup, bringing it to his lips. I imagine that he isn't thinking about much else.

"Mr. Anastasi?"

"Yeah?"

"How are you going to get well enough to leave if you don't talk to me?"

He faces me, gets up, then stomps out of the dayroom. He has on big, unlaced work boots. The laces flop around crazily in all directions and slap the linoleum tiles as he walks along.

His departure doesn't come as a surprise to me. Ever since I started to meet with him two weeks ago, our time is up when I ask a question and he walks out. I consider it our ritual.

I start to rise. Christina comes over and presses down on my shoulder until I sit back down. We started going out together two days ago. We talk about last night, and tonight, and the upcoming weekend. Naturally, she has a great laugh, et cetera.

Since I started seeing a nurse on the unit, I've been more relaxed about my work. It's like I have a secret ally at staff meetings. I don't feel so alone.

"Are you still having problems with Eddie?" Christina refers to Mr. Anastasi.

"Yup."

"Look, I grew up with guys just like him. He's a pussycat, really. It's just this macho Italian thing. My older brother's the same way."

"So what do I do?"

"There's nothing you can do. That's just the way he is. I mean, he figures it's better to act tough than to be crazy like the other patients up here. He's not about to sit down and talk about his feelings with you. I'll bet he didn't even talk about his feelings with his girlfriend!"

"Mmm."

"But I think you're doing the right thing by sitting with him and having coffee. At least that way he gets used to seeing you every morning."

Christina suggests that I gather history about Mr. Anastasi by reviewing his chart again, with an eye toward finding data in the history that might be useful in developing a treatment plan. If he won't tell me about himself, perhaps the documents that accompanied him from Monterey State Hospital will.

"And don't skim this time," she admonishes. "Concentrate. I know you're feeling overwhelmed, but if you do it right the first time, you won't have to repeat the work."

The patients' charts are suspended upside-down between two parallel bars in a wheeled metal cart kept in the nurses' station. They are open to staff, residents, interns, medical and social work students, outside consultants who come into the hospital, and health insurers. Mr. Anastasi's chart is nearly as thick as the white pages of a phone book.

It becomes clear from my review that this man has behaved violently his whole life. It is documented that during his adolescence he regularly beat up strangers in bars, was often seen drunk and staggering in public, and while on the job threatened and fought with co-workers. As an adult, he continued these behaviors and added to them so severe and terrifying an incident of beating up his girlfriend that police had to intervene. Subsequent to the attack, she broke off their relationship.

At the same time, the documents in his chart show that he finished high school by the time he was eighteen. He has always had friends and family who try to rescue him from jams. He has worked pretty steadily for the same employer on an assembly line in a candy factory for about ten years (although it is a first cousin who may have been more tolerant of odd family behavior than an outsider would be). He has had no major medical problems or illnesses other than the alcoholism. Prior to the current admission and its precipitant, he had never been placed in a psychiatric hospital or put in jail. Since the break-up, he has managed to live alone in an apartment without disturbing his neighbors.

The criminal offense that he committed was a traffic violation: he was stopped by the police for running a stop sign, found to be combative, and taken in. He became violent and psychotic while in the holding cell and was transferred for evaluation to Monterey State Hospital.

It's about now that I think that Christina may be somewhat mistaken about Mr. Anastasi. His problems are anything but ordinary. For example, the fact that there is nothing apparent in his history to explain his current predicament suggests to me something insidious. His alcoholism helps me to understand the violence and poor judgment, but it does not explain his bizarre affect, his intermittent psychosis, or his silence. The next morning I return to the source for answers.

Mr. Anastasi pries loose the thin white plastic lid of the coffee container. I do the same with mine. At the same time, we place them on the linoleum floor. He sips. So I sip. He takes out a cigarette and lights up. But I don't smoke. Halfway to the filter, I perk up. I hope that I can win him over through enthusiasm, through sheer force of will.

"Ah, Mr. Anastasi, what a day. Have you been outside? It's hot. It's a perfect Indian summer day."

He nods his head up and down a little bit, almost imperceptibly, like he's been tricked into doing something he'd rather not do.

"I been stuck in here because you won't let me out." His eyelids get lower and he moves his lips almost to a pout. "How about it? How about letting me out? Perfect summer day, huh?"

At least we're talking, I figure. If he can take it, so can I.

"Maybe."

"Depends, huh?"

"Depends."

"Like if I'm a good boy, right?"

"Mmm."

"Yeah."

"Uh huh."

"So?"

"So what?"

"So how do I get outta here? What're the magic words? I, Eddie Anastasi, do solemnly swear to do what you tell me to do? Is that it?"

"You're in a hospital, Eddie. There's certain rules you have to follow. What can I tell you?"

He gets up and stomps out.

After three weeks of this ceremony, Tom and the entire nursing staff, except for Christina, my loyalist, decide that it's time once again to prod me into more meaningful action. I am told to get a consultation on Mr. Anastasi.

The hospital has various consultation services, including psychopharmacology, forensic psychiatry, and psychological testing. Each consult service offers expert opinion and is made up of senior staff, a chief resident (if it is medical), and sometimes research fellows outside the training programs as such. Because Tom thinks that medication could help Mr. Anastasi, he suggests I get a psychopharm. consult; he also thinks that Mr. Anastasi may have very limited intelligence and suggests I set up psychological testing to see if this is true. I fill out the appropriate referral forms and with Alice Duerler, my med. backup, prepare a history to present to the psychopharmacology consultation team.

It is at this moment that Mr. Anastasi takes a sudden, wildly unexpected nosedive.

He and another patient are caught making love in her bed. She has appeared to be extremely psychotic for most of her life, and everyone is surprised that Eddie would pair off with her. We all

thought he was healthier than that. A patient's choice of lovers
in the hospital is revealing diagnostically. Who they love helps
to reveal their self-perception. An extremely disturbed person,
for example, is likely to form a relationship with someone equally
disturbed. Eddie's lover is schizophrenic. Does this mean that
he is schizophrenic, too? It becomes a question in the minds of
staff and trainees who attend to him. In the meantime, the immediate problem also needs to be dealt with decisively, since
patient contact is strictly taboo.

Eddie is brought before a small assembly of doctors, nurses,
trainees, M.H.A.'s. I tell him that his behavior is "inappropriate." What happened between him and this woman can't happen
again. He says, "OK" at once, but then he starts muttering
curses at me and the M.H.A.'s and the nursing staff, saying that
we're all assholes and that we're taking away his freedom and
that we have no right to tell him who to fuck or when to fuck or
how to fuck, and before you know it, he's lifted a wooden chair
over his head and is charging toward our stupid little group with
the apparent intent of clobbering us all. He is stopped momen-
tarily by Anton and Rashid, who try to restrain him.

Immediately, a nurse runs to a phone to call a code green.
This means that every available male staff, trainee, and employee in the hospital has to stop whatever he's doing and charge
to our side in case a show of force is necessary either to intim-
idate or physically overpower a patient. Soon we're a crowd of
about thirty guys forming a semicircle that pushes Mr. Anastasi
into a corner. The chief of security, a middle-aged man with a
huge gut and Coke-bottle glasses, shows up and breaks up the
riot with two young goons, whose necks are festooned with
braided gold chains.

"OK, OK, back off." Then he whispers into his walkie-
talkie, which he handles like a weapon. He also has a revolver
belted around his waist, in case talk is cheap. "The code is
over."

Everyone relaxes and strolls to the doors of the unit, big
skeleton keys in hand. I stay close to the cops and Mr. Anastasi.

"Come on now, come on," says the chief. He coaxes Mr.

Anastasi like he's a loose, dumb circus tiger. "Let's go, come on. They ain't gonna hurt ya."

We stay in this temperate zone. Mr. Anastasi is led along, held on both sides to the seclusion room, where he is locked in. Tom documents the incident to prove that no other option was available to us. Mr. Anastasi calms down and walks to a corner of the room where he slouches and sulks. It is while he is in seclusion, sometime early Monday morning, that he has a grand mal seizure.

I am among the first to discover this. When I walk up to the tiny window of the seclusion room, just after eight A.M., holding two Styrofoam cups in my hands, a slim maroon appointment book tucked between my arm and body, I see Mr. Anastasi lying on his belly, naked, still, covered in his shit.

The door is unlocked and he is cleaned and covered up to the neck with a freshly laundered white sheet. Then he's lifted onto a stretcher that is carried off the unit by a pair of M.H.A.'s. Soon Mr. Anastasi is transferred to one of the medical hospitals across the street. While there, he is evaluated neurologically. He recovers in twenty-four hours. When well enough, he is transferred back to Comm. Mental.

It doesn't take the psychopharm. team long to decide that Mr. Anastasi may have a seizure disorder that ought to be treated with anticonvulsants. They hesitate about the diagnosis because he has no history of seizures. And except for the chronic alcoholism, it isn't altogether clear what might have caused this one. To cover their bet, they also suggest a trial of antipsychotic medication.

When the results from neurology come back, they confirm the suspicions of the psychopharm. service: In addition to whatever other psychological problems he may have, Mr. Anastasi is diagnosed with temporal lobe epilepsy, also known as TLE. The diagnosis is just starting to be in vogue in psychiatric circles. The way Alice, my med. backup, explains it to me, TLE indicates a brain abnormality in the temporal lobe. This abnormality is sometimes at the root of an individual's otherwise inexplicable rage, impulsivity, moodiness, recalcitrance, and even psychosis. At last, we have an answer!

Predictably, however, Mr. Anastasi refuses to cooperate with most of the arrangements we make for him. He agrees only to take medication to control his seizures. For a while, this becomes the focus of his treatment: making certain he is medication compliant, trying to convince him to take antipsychotics, and encouraging him to cooperate with psychological testing.

I fail on all three accounts. Mr. Anastasi soon complains of the drowsiness that accompanies the medicine, and rejects it. He also becomes reclusive. He sits by himself in the dayroom. He walks out when I walk in. He stiffens up, clenches his fists, and glowers at the M.H.A.'s when they get closer than a foot away from him.

He also begins to talk to himself about things that don't make sense to anybody else. For example, he says, "I'm a mind reader," or, "I have secret powers," or, "I can destroy you just by thinking about it." We are confused by these remarks and behavioral changes. Nothing seems to explain them. Perhaps when a human being is robbed of his physical powers, and made helpless, he begins to believe more in the unseen, a force that is his alone, and that cannot be taken away from him.

"He's beginning to look to me like a train wreck," says Tom in supervision with me. He lights a cigarette. He handles it inexpertly, like someone trying to start or quit. The only time I ever see Tom smoke is during supervision. He seems jittery off the unit. He takes a puff, then holds the cigarette as far away as possible. He explains, "The term means that maybe Mr. Anastasi is one of those people who has an incredible array of all kinds of problems, medical and psychological. He's really a mess. Nothing but trouble since the beginning." He pauses to take another reluctant puff. "Look, we have to decide if we can treat him. And if he won't give us his cooperation, then we need to get it."

The message is clear: guardianship. In days, I have drawn up the necessary papers. I have prepared to state my case before the judge. If I have learned one thing from my own therapy, which I started less than a month ago, it's that I have to get compulsive about doing the work if I am to succeed at my internship. I have to do what I'm told because otherwise it won't get done and I will get into trouble. I have to stop acting out my anxiety.

The hearing is held in the same room we used to send Mr. Plummer up the river. The judge is duly impressed by Mr. Anastasi's display. In a few minutes, it's over.

I expect the situation to improve at once, but of course it doesn't. Mr. Anastasi becomes mute. He postures wildly with his arms and legs. Occasionally, he takes the medicine given to him, not enough to have any impact, but just enough to avoid having to get I.M. injections.

We don't know what to do next. Can we transfer him back to a strictly medical hospital where his epilepsy can be studied and treated? Can we return him to Monterey? Before we decide, he starts to cooperate with my treatment plan.

He agrees to take his medicine—but *only* if Christina gives it to him. I don't like it. But Christina thinks the request is innocent enough. "I'm a big girl," she says. And the rest of the staff agrees because "it's worth a try."

So once in the morning and once at the end of her day, Christina practically skips into the dayroom to hand Eddie his pills and a cup of water. He swallows them and sips the water. When she turns her back to him, he looks at her hungrily until she's out of sight.

"How do you feel about Eddie's crush?" I ask Christina. She is staying the night.

"On me or on you?"

"Me? You!"

"Well, he seems awfully fond of us both. Why else would he want to flirt with me other than to send you some kind of message?"

"Because you're incredibly beautiful and remind him of Italian girls he used to date in high school."

"Scott, there are other Italian girls on the unit. I'll admit I am the most beautiful. Do you really think so. . . ?"

"Yes. Yes, I do."

"Why, thank you."

Nora hugs Nick Charles. Then we get on with it.

"I think," Christina continues, "I think he's trying to tell you that he's still a guy. He's trying to take your girl away."

"Well, I won't let him!"

"Eddie's your patient, not your rival."

"Says who?"

"Says me."

"I see."

"You do."

As a result of this conversation and others about Eddie's crush on her, Christina and I decide to behave toward one another like young professionals while we are on the unit. We make no displays of affection and say as little as possible to one another. The only one who seems to be affected negatively by this is me.

Mr. Anastasi is emboldened. Does he imagine that things have cooled between Christina and me? He invites her to sit beside him while he has a smoke. He talks to her about his special powers. Diagnostically, by his choice of Christina, is this a sign that Mr. Anastasi is getting better?

At first, this appears to be true. Perhaps Mr. Anastasi loves Christina for the same reasons I love her: she is deliberate, calm, and funny. Most importantly, she is not afraid of anger. Unfortunately, her acceptance and soothing don't satisfy him. He also wants to embrace her.

Soon he's acting worse than ever. Sitting with Christina isn't enough, it isn't enough, he wants more. Don't I know it? He stops taking medicine. He threatens M.H.A.'s and male staff. I start avoiding him, even cutting down the number of times I pop in to see how he's doing.

The staff consensus is that it's time to send him back to Monterey. Tom and I call Dan Gutman, the chief psychologist there, to see about a transfer. Dr. Gutman isn't surprised by our call. He figured it could go either way. He knows that Eddie is difficult. But he doesn't want him back.

"We're a facility for the criminally insane. And unless Eddie performs a criminal act, he doesn't belong here."

"What about the violent threats?"

"But has he done anything? No. Look, call me each time there's any sort of incident. We'll evaluate the situation as it changes. If we have to take him back, we'll take him back. But not right now. Let's give him another chance."

Little incidents pile up. Mr. Anastasi steals a pair of shoes. He throws cups of coffee on the dayroom floor. He shoves somebody out of the way.

"He's trying to tell us by his behavior that he doesn't want to be here," says Tom. "He wants to go back to Monterey."

"Why?"

"Maybe he feels safer in a more contained environment. The rules are clearer. The expectations are limited. And there're fewer women to stimulate him. I don't think he can control himself when he's sexually aroused."

Tom's impression proves to be completely accurate. A few days later Eddie attempts to rape a female patient. We can finally make a case to Gutman that it's time for Eddie Anastasi to return to Monterey State Hospital.

We're all glad to see him go.

It is a long and dreary winter in Boston. Christina and I have broken up amicably so that she can return to her ex-husband and I can be reconciled with my ex-girlfriend. On New Year's Day, my ex and I break if off, finally. Now I'm seeing a variety of people, including Suzanne, a midwestern farm girl whose first question to me when we are alone is, "What's it like being Jewish?" Well, it's not such a dreary winter, after all, but it is chaotic. Since breaking up finally with my ex-girlfriend, all I want to do is have fun. I'm a lot happier with the final resolution, although given how low I was feeling before New Year's

Day, that sure isn't saying much. Perhaps I was right the first time. It is a long and dreary winter.

That's when Mr. Anastasi comes back into my life. After three months at Monterey, he is his old tough-guy, sans psychosis self. Gutman wants him out of there. But Tom is convinced that his return will be a repetition of what happened the first time. A compromise is reached. Tom and I agree to visit Eddie Anastasi at Monterey. Gutman will interview him, put him through his paces, and if we're satisfied by the behavior, we agree to take him back. If not, then no deal.

The final mile to the hospital takes us through wetlands and empty fields. A farmhouse and barn appear on the right. A man goes by in a tractor. Two big men step beside him. A big wheel splatters mud on their faces, caps, and long black aprons. Two hundred yards up ahead, there's the old brick building that houses the chronic population, most of whom are violent sexual offenders. Beyond it is a pentagon with new offices and cells; in its center is the prison yard.

Tom and I introduce ourselves to an armed guard in the pentagon. He checks our names off a typed list held to a clipboard. We proceed to security: no aliases, no weapons, no drugs, no alcohol. We pass through a series of thick, electronically controlled doors. We are led down several passageways.

We meet Gutman in his office. He's wearing a suit. Handshakes all around, a few polite, collegial words between him and Tom, and then he telephones somebody to have Mr. Anastasi brought in. We can see part of the yard from the office. Our man steps into view. He's wearing prison work clothes.

"Eddie, I believe you remember Dr. Downes and Dr. Haas." He leads him toward us, and we all shake hands. He waves him to a seat. "How are you doing, Eddie?"

"Good."

"Why don't you tell Dr. Downes and Dr. Haas a little bit about what you've been up to?"

He tells us about the college-type classes he's been attending, the basketball team, the movies he's seen. He talks without feeling. Has Mr. Anastasi become a young professional, too?

Suddenly, Gutman interrupts and gets ugly. I've seen this routine before. The smart guy slums to show he can play both sides. He talks dirty, acts tough. Is he showing off to us, too?

"Now, Eddie, I know you want to go home, right? Am I right?"

"Yeah, you're right."

"But I don't want any bullshit. You know I can smell bullshit a mile away."

"Yeah, I know that."

"So you're not fucking with me, right? You're not fucking around?"

"No."

"Are you going to behave yourself at Comm. Mental? You're not going to fuck it up for yourself again?"

"No."

"Because you know what'll happen, right? What'll happen? Tell me. Come on. Tell Dr. Downes and Dr. Haas, too."

"I get sent back here."

"Thataboy. Now for God's sake, don't fuck it up."

Gutman then asks his boy to recite the initial treatment plan so there is no way that he can say that he doesn't get it. Anastasi sounds like a first-grader saying the Pledge of Allegiance. What's that make me?

Gutman is specific about the no-no's of violent or inappropriate behavior and about drinking. He turns to us and asks if we have any questions, but everything seems to have been covered by the display. Eddie is told he can stand up. He is told to shake our hands. Then he is led away by a guard who's been waiting outside the door, just in case Eddie doesn't follow the script.

"Well, he certainly seems like a different Eddie Anastasi than the one I knew," says Tom.

"You have to be firm with him," says Gutman. "He needs to know what the limits are."

We have no choice but to accept this changed man. On the way back to Boston, Tom and I discuss the meaning of Monterey to Mr. Anastasi. Perhaps he feels better off being treated like someone who broke the law rather than as a mental patient. There's more dignity in it.

Back at Comm. Mental, the staff prepares for the worst. We're all resolved to boot Eddie out at his first transgression. When he strides back in, however, everyone is very friendly. We want him to see that we're willing to take him back if he plays ball. It's not hypocrisy so much as distance that we're trying to create. The man seems unpredictable, and if it is one thing the staff doesn't like, it's not knowing what comes next.

This time around the consensus is that Mr. Anastasi needs clear instructions and a treatment plan he can figure out and follow. I draw one up:

TREATMENT PLAN FOR EDDIE ANASTASI

1. Patient has dayroom privileges for twenty-four hours. If he is above suspicion, he then has:

2. Full unit privileges for twenty-four hours. If he is above suspicion, he then has:

3. Full in-patient hospital privileges for ninety-six hours. If he is above suspicion, he then has:

4. Day-hospital privileges with full restrictions for forty-eight hours. If he is above suspicion, he then has:

5. Full day-hospital privileges with Boisvert Inn (a shelter set up in the hospital gymnasium for homeless day-hospital patients). If patient does well in the day hospital (is above suspicion), outside living will be considered.

One copy of this plan is given to Mr. Anastasi, other copies are circulated to staff assigned to his case, and one copy is placed in his chart.

Mr. Anastasi behaves compliantly from beginning to end. He is not psychotic. He doesn't hassle Christina or even show any interest in her. There are no reported seizures. He looks spent. All he talks about, repetitively, in a monotonic voice, is his desire to go home, get a job, and start his life over. It sounds like he is parroting someone else's words. But his absence of feeling is rarely a topic of discussion between staff. We're glad, simply, that he is less trouble this time around, whatever the reason may be for the change.

Over a period of five months, he progresses steadily through the various stages of my treatment plan until, finally, he is a day-hospital patient sleeping in the Boisvert Inn. By the time my internship ends, we are meeting twice weekly in my office to talk concretely about his finding a job, meeting a woman, and getting his apartment back into shape. He still speaks without feeling, and there is an aura of guardedness about him. But again, the main issues have been addressed. He is no longer scary or threatening. He cooperates with treatment. He plans ahead.

Three weeks after my internship ends, I learn that Eddie Anastasi never makes it out.

ABOUT HUNGER

New admissions are assigned to psychology interns or psychiatry residents on the basis of a rotation. When a young woman named Fay Shepard is admitted one afternoon, I am next on the list, and she is assigned to me. Fay is different from anyone I've ever met before.

As I have come to expect by this time, the facts about her—what is said to be true—are skimpy. She is from Arizona, the only scion of a ranching dynasty that is three generations in the making. She finished high school near Phoenix and then decided to stay at home and to work locally. Her parents were disappointed. She had always been an A student; as a junior and senior, she displayed particular strengths in mathematics, biology, chemistry, and physics. They had imagined that she would attend Smith or Mount Holyoke, or maybe even Radcliffe.

Instead, Fay worked for a couple of months as a check-out girl at a convenience store before quitting abruptly. There has never been a boyfriend in the picture, and she's always been the sort of girl who likes to be on her own rather than with a group of kids.

"Fay has always been a very independent young lady," says mother via the telephone when I call her for history and opinion. "And stubborn, too. When she makes up her mind, she is the only one who can change it."

One day, sometime between the holidays of Thanksgiving and Christmas, Fay climbed the stairs from the family den in the basement and strolled into the kitchen-cum-patio where mom was having a cup of coffee while reading the morning paper. Fay said, "I am the reincarnation of Joan of Arc." She was calm about her discovery. She confided: "I've figured it out from deciphering secret coded messages on the TV."

"Oh?" exclaims mom, more as a way to relieve tension than as a question or a note of surprise. She returns cup to saucer, folds newspaper, and asks daughter to sit down. When Fay takes a seat, mother gets up and walks to the wall phone and begins to dial. So far there's been no expression of feeling, nor has there been any physical contact between them. While mom talks into the mouthpiece, never taking her eyes off of Fay, the girl stays mute and still.

Mother arranges to have Fay seen by a local psychiatrist recommended to her by the family's physician. Fay worsens in a few weeks. She loses fifteen pounds, begins to vomit up meals, and finally refuses to eat. She is increasingly preoccupied by whispering voices of her dead ancestors, who talk vaguely about poisoning her. She prefers to stay in her bedroom most of the time. She says that she feels safer there. The family terminates Fay's treatment with the psychiatrist. (As my work with patients' families intensifies, the social workers' terms make more sense to me. Their understanding of patients as part of a family in distress keeps me from isolating the mentally ill person from the context in which their terrible predicament developed.)

Their doctor now advises placing Fay in a private psychiatric institution in Houston he's heard or read about. But since they can't recall anything like this ever having happened before to them or to anyone they know even remotely, the family is afraid. Fay's parents wish someone could make the decision for them. No one knows what to do.

Father's younger sister, Maxine, steps in. She tells the family to permit Fay to move in with her. She will supervise all of Fay's activities. She will have her seen by a top-notch psychiatrist. The family sends her to Boston on the first available flight. Maxine is in her late thirties and is a doctoral candidate at the Harvard Divinity School. She lives in exclusive Beacon Hill, a quiet old area in the center of the city with lots of charm, shade provided by brick buildings, quaint, narrow alleyways, views of the Charles River, the Boston Common.

Ten days after Fay arrives, however, the plan is jettisoned. She has swallowed a bottle of cough syrup and a handful of aspirin in an effort to convince others that she intends to kill herself. She is sick to her stomach when Maxine brings her in to Comm. Mental via Mass. General, where she had first been medically treated and cleared. The family chooses our public hospital because father does not want to spend the $350–$600 *per day* it costs for private hospitalization. Fay's health insurance is inadequate.

On my first encounter with Fay, I see that her body is taut. She also looks as if she has a mask over her face that conveys astonishment, confusion, curiosity, and certainty all at the same time. What is she hiding from us? What does she really look like? Or is this her interior? Has she turned herself inside out?

An early session takes place in Fay's bedroom on the locked unit. (She has refused to be with other patients in the dayroom, but won't say why.) I lift a wooden chair by its back to within two feet of the neat mattress. Fay is sitting up. I sit down. Her posture stays rigid. She keeps her hands in a position over her bent knees which makes them appear to be useless. Fay has been in the hospital less than a day. I ask her how she feels right now.

"OK," she answers. Her tinny voice makes it hard to hear her. Maybe she doesn't want to be heard, or is used to being the sort of person people find it hard to understand or must strain to hear properly. She looks up at me for just a second, then darts a look down again at those hands. She shrugs her shoulders swiftly. "I don't know."

"How do you feel about being in the hospital?"

"I don't have any feelings."

I won't quit. I ask more questions. In a hospital, pertinent information about the patient must be gathered quickly. In one hour, I will lead a discussion at team meeting on Fay's predicament. Within twenty-four hours, I must write what I know of her history into a chart. By the end of the week, I may have to help present her to Tom at a staff meeting. (All new admissions are presented to staff within days after they have been admitted.) Fay doesn't express much awareness of why she is here, or why others are so concerned about her. She is genuinely uncertain.

Q: What problems brought you here?

A: I tried to kill myself.

Q: How come?

A: I don't know.

Q: Had you felt this way before?

A: Off and on. Yes.

Q: When did you first feel like dying?

A: I don't know. I don't remember. When I was twelve, I guess. I don't know.

Q: What happened when you were twelve that led you to feel that way?

A: Nothing. I don't know. I can't remember.

Q: Have you ever spoken to a psychologist, psychiatrist, or social worker before?

A: My mother took me to Dr. K. before I came here.

Q: When was that?

A: After I told her about the messages on the TV.

Q: She didn't believe you?

A: No.

Q: What do you think now about the messages on the TV?

A: I don't know. I think it's better not to say anything.

Q: Because?

A: Because no one believes me.

Q: What's that like? Not being believed? Distrusted?

A: I'm used to it.

Q: Oh?

A: Can we talk about something else?

Q: Tell me about Dr. K.

A: He was OK. He was nice, I guess.

Q: But he didn't help you.

A: No.

Q: What sort of help do you feel you need?

A: I don't know. Maybe if people would leave me alone . . .

Fay shows no feelings that are easily recognizable to me during the inquiry. When I sit with her and try to imagine what she is experiencing, I feel plenty of emptiness. This creates a union of sorts between us, but it does not lead to greater understanding, nor does it lessen Fay's pain. Or does it?

I have to accept Fay *on her terms* if we are to progress. So we sit for a long while in silence. Her compatriots on the unit express themselves similarly. A passage in *Malone Dies*, a novel by Samuel Beckett, helps to explain how I see their predicament: "They had no conversation properly speaking. They made use of the spoken word in much the same way as the guard of a train makes use of his flags, or of his lantern."

How can I connect to her? She starts to rock back and forth. I can't stop talking, and it's still in that robotic, intense, and directed way that excludes much in the way of spontaneity or warmth. There must be an easier way to find out what I need to know about Fay, but I don't know what it is. That's how little I know about people at this point in the internship, and in my life.

Fay doesn't answer any of my questions. She's too preoccupied. The interview is over when I get up.

I keep waiting for Fay to tell me about her life. A lot of time goes by before I realize that she has been telling me about herself all along.

She can't talk about herself so she uses her body to convey her feelings. Knowing this, however, does not bridge the canyon between us. But perhaps it can. Perhaps, as usual, I am in too great a hurry to diagnose the problem, solve it, and move on to the next patient. Because as Fay lives in her body, I live in my mind. My therapist points out to me that I have developed the habit of turning my feelings into thoughts. I create structures to codify and assemble the amorphousness around and within me. I am impatient when faced with a novelty that does not conform readily to the forms I have created already. Fay's disguise is her body, and mine is my intellect. I will be better off by dwelling on her feelings rather than attempting to identify and placate them. After all, it must have taken her a very long time to develop this identity that frightens her family so much. I ought to respect the power and resilience of her imagination, and its ability to resolve conflict, however much is destroyed in that process. I ought to respect myself more, too.

Perhaps Fay and I can connect through our common habit of magical transformation. She turns her body into the world. I turn my feelings into words. The two of us are made more alone in these ways. Have I learned this from sitting in silence with her? Can we share and believe in the strength of solitude?

Unfortunately, the requirements of the hospital outweigh the need of the patient to embody disorder and the need of the intern to intellectualize it. Meditation is OK, but it must conform to the strictures of a treatment plan.

When I discuss Fay at team meeting soon after her admission, the focus of proposed intervention becomes almost immediately: FOOD. MEDICATION. Everyone agrees that Fay is a diagnostic mystery, but while we try to figure out whether her psychotic behavior is symptomatic of a personality disorder, a schizophrenia, a major depression, post-traumatic stress, or an eating disorder (or some combination of these diagnostic categories), we must keep her alive. Presently, she refuses meals, or eats to excess before vomiting it all up in a bathroom sink.

She says that she doesn't want to die, but she isn't doing enough to stay alive. She depends upon others for safety and well-being, but denies that she needs anyone or their help.

In the poem *Leaves of Grass*, Walt Whitman accepts contradiction as natural:

> *Do I contradict myself?*
> *Very well then, I contradict myself,*
> *(I am large, I contain multitudes).*

I am not free to see things this way, because I work in a hospital where in order for there to be a cure, there must also be a sickness. And rather than accept Fay's contradictions as a way for her to orient herself, however faulty that compass, the team, with my ready assent, calls for a finely detailed daily schedule that Fay can put in a pocket and carry around with her, and a trial of Haldol, an antipsychotic medication. The schedule emphasizes the need for her to eat and drink like a normal person, to attend the groups on the unit, and to stay out of her bedroom during daytime hours. In addition, Jamie Armstrong, a very thin social worker whom I am especially fond of, and whom I admire for the strength of her intellect, will work with Maxine and the family. I am to conduct individual psychotherapy with Fay four times weekly for thirty-minute sessions in the mornings.

The plan is first disrupted when Fay hoards the Haldol and then swallows the stash. Although it is nearly impossible to take a lethal dosage of this medication, her action has the desired effects. We share in her desperation. We recognize her frailty. We believe she is sad. We are very frightened.

Fay cannot explain why she took the overdose. "I'm not suicidal," she answers matter-of-factly, and in response to a direct question. "I don't know why I did it." Reluctantly, she agrees not to try to kill herself again. Alice adds an antidepressant medication to her regimen.

In the meantime, there is the matter of diet. Fay still won't eat any meals. Her day begins with a weigh-in on the tall scale in the examination room adjacent to the nurses' station. A nurse records each loss on a chart held to a clipboard. Fay will waste away unless we stop her.

Accordingly, the treatment team decides to share Fay's preoccupation with food. We focus on this problem for several reasons. The matter is urgent. If Fay does not start to eat, she will starve to death. The matter is obvious. It is unlike the diagnostic mystery enshrouding the etiology and nature of her psychosis and depression. The matter is familiar. For years, many of the women and some of the men on the staff and among the trainees have starved themselves or vomited their food to lose weight and appear thin. Since I started treatment of Fay, at least five women staff or trainees have told me that they consider themselves to have been anorectic and/or bulemic when they were college undergraduates.

How does it feel for Fay to have the staff of a major teaching hospital quite concerned about what and how often she eats?

She is a very polite listener. For example, one morning Katherine, one of the psychiatry residents, stops by to offer support to Fay by telling her about her junior year at Wellesley College when she dieted and binged and lost a tremendous amount of weight until she found a "terrific therapist" at the student counseling services who got her "back on track."

"And you're better now?" asks Fay, meekly.

"I'm much better," answers Katherine.

"Oh," she says.

Katherine's confession to Fay annoys me because it seems motivated more by a need to talk about herself rather than a desire to help the patient. Tom concurs, and there are no more staff confessions to Fay. She is now more alone than ever.

There is only so much that you can say about food. Fay knows by now that we all want her to eat meals instead of refusing them or vomiting them up. Having established this with her, I feel it's OK to start talking with Fay about her predicament on the unit. Is her refusal to eat a metaphor for a feeling or thought she finds so intolerable that she must embody it? What is the impact of the starvation upon others and herself?

Q: What do you think about all day in your room?
A: I wonder what will happen to me.

Q: And how does that make you feel?
A: Alone.

Fay still won't spend time in the dayroom. Her removal from the hub of activity suggests the possibility that she becomes frightened when surrounded by madness. Diagnostically, this is often a good indicator that the individual who is suffering has a greater awareness of pain than someone whose whole life is organized around it and who can no longer imagine living without the pain—like most of the patients wandering aimlessly or talking to themselves in the in-patient dayrooms.

Q: Have you spoken to any of the other patients?
A: Yes. A little.
Q: Have you made any friends?
A: No.
Q: Do you like any people in particular on the unit?
A: No. Not really.

Who knows what is wrong with Fay? She is not telling any of us directly. She is almost completely disengaged. When she does talk freely, it's typically to tell us about the prophecies of Jeane Dixon, parapsychology, astral planes, reincarnation, and the lives of the saints. Her affect is bland or sullen. She looks like a wax figure that has been brought to life without having been given any feelings to guide its actions.

It's no wonder we talk to her about food; this other stuff is scary and incomprehensible! Now food, there's something we can all understand and appreciate! Perhaps Fay has chosen a language to convey her life out of deference to the feelings of others. She talks about food because she wants us to understand. But understand what? That she's been hungry so long that she's lost her appetite?

We need more data on this person. Weeks have gone by, but we still don't know just what we're treating. I haven't been able to get information from the patient or from Maxine. Jamie's phone calls to the family become more insistent. She also gets complete medical and school records sent to her.

One morning at team meeting Jamie presents what she has learned about Fay. There is no history or suspicion of sexual abuse. Prior to this episode of psychotically depressed behavior, Fay has never been seen to be abnormal. The anorexia and bulemia are recent phenomena.

"What are we going to do?" asks Jamie. "Alice has her on antidepressants and antipsychotics. You meet with her almost every day. She still won't attend groups, and she's barely eating. What are we doing for her? Does she still belong here?"

"She definitely needs to be here," I say. "She's still acutely suicidal."

"Well, OK, I agree, but family is concerned about her. What can I say to reassure them?"

"I don't know," I say.

"I don't know either," Alice says.

"Great," says Jamie. Her humor is typically acerbic, biting, like my own. We bite the hand that feeds us. But our self-sufficiency is an illusion; we are dependent upon that hand even though we act to deny it all of the time. Fay can't deny it. "I'll just tell them that we don't know what's wrong with daughter, and that we're not sure how long she needs to be here. Terrific."

The fact that we don't understand Fay is not exceptional. Many of the people admitted as patients to Comm. Mental present themselves to us in a way that makes interpretation, diagnosis, and treatment of their dysfunctional behavior—even up to the time that they are discharged from the hospital—largely a matter of observing an intervention that enables the individual to function better and then making this thing the linchpin of the treatment. For example, Fay may be given a potpourri of treatments: antidepressants; antipsychotics; Lithium; anticonvulsants; group psychotherapies; movement therapies; occupational therapies; expressive therapies; individual psychodynamic psychotherapy. The treatment may lead to the diagnosis of the problem, rather than the other way around, as is customary in most other fields of medicine. For example, if a patient responds well to Lithium, he can be diagnosed as manic-depressive. If a course of antipsychotic medication calms him down, he may be diagnosed as having a disorder with psychosis. The patient's response to the intervention often leads to the diagnosis, an improper, upside-down approach virtually unique to mental health, and one that separates it from other branches of medical practice, which have more precise tools for diagnosing *physical* ailments (for example, X-rays, blood tests, EKGs).

It is Fay's extreme bad luck to have a disorder that is not clearly amenable to any of our interventions.

Maxine's impatience with our lack of progress turns out to be the catalyst in Fay's case. She meets with Jamie, Alice, and me in Jamie's office and demands to know how she can be of help. As usual, she's dressed beautifully. In fact, we all are. It's no wonder that Fay communicates through her body; she has observed that it is part of our vocabulary. She just wants to take the matter to its obvious conclusion. And we won't let her.

The gist of Maxine's visit is that she wants to take Fay on little day trips outside the hospital to cheer her up. "Boston is a beautiful city," she says, "and I know Fay's very sick, but getting out with me should help to cheer her up."

There's no reason not to allow this to happen. If Maxine can guarantee her safety, and Fay agrees not to run off and try and kill herself, then why not? The one proviso comes from Jamie, who insists that Fay attend groups and eat regularly for one week before being handed this gift. We all agree it's a good idea.

Although Fay does not explain her decision, and still refuses to discuss her hunger, she begins to appear more frequently in the dayroom. She starts to eat meals and even gains a little bit of weight. She attends a few of the groups. Not that any of this more acceptable behavior helps to explain the peculiarity of her thinking or prior unwillingness to eat in an ordinary way. What will satisfy Fay?

■　　■　　■　　■

Maxine tells Fay that she will take her anywhere she wants to
go. Fay proposes that they go together to the zoo. They drive to
the Stoneham Zoo on the north shore beyond the city and tour
the exhibits. Does Fay take pleasure from seeing ravenous animals pacing, caged and hungry? Who knows? That's my facile
interpretation, but what is Fay's point of view? She won't say.

After the zoo, Fay suggests abruptly that Maxine return her
to the hospital. Maxine is flustered and hurt, but Fay has made
up her mind. Along the way, Maxine proposes that they stop for
a quick lunch. They order hamburgers at a fast-food outlet. Fay
eats hers, but then sickens at table and throws up, stumbling, on
her knees, braced against the floor with outstretched arm and
palm, en route to the toilet. She's practically in tears as she tells
Maxine how embarrassed she is. She hadn't meant to throw up.
She couldn't help it. Maxine says, "Never mind" and cleans her
with a beach towel she keeps in the trunk of the car.

Once in Boston, Maxine suggests that they go clothes shopping at Bonwit's. Fay is reluctant, but Maxine says it will be
fun. Fay doesn't fight her. In the store she refuses to try anything
on until Maxine promises not to look at her in the new clothes.
She selects two skirts, a blouse, and a dress. Later on Maxine
sees that the clothes are two sizes too big. Is this how big Fay
would like to be? Does she imagine that she is that big already?
Is she afraid of becoming so big? Does she know that the clothes
are too big?

Back on the unit, Fay begins to establish a routine. She eats
regularly and attends her groups. At the same time, she acts
more clearly psychotic. For example, she talks almost exclusively about having been reincarnated, about astral projection,
and about out-of-body experiences. Her body, its sacrifice, is
still the focal point. When I talk to her about other concerns,
she won't say more than "OK," or "all right," or "fine." I
have no idea from these expressions whether or not she means
that her life is good or bad.

Every Saturday, Maxine arrives punctually to take her niece
out for the afternoon. She and Fay tour the city: antique fairs,

the Busch-Reisinger Museum at Harvard, tea at the Ritz-Carlton, Chinatown. They conspire to act as if nothing is wrong.

But Maxine's pleasure turns into concern when she, too, observes that Fay has started to "talk crazy" all of the time.

"She seemed better off when we left her alone," she says.

We confront Fay with her delusions. Initially, she tries to justify them to us. When she observes that no one is convinced of their merit, she clams up. She also starts to refuse meals again. Accepting Fay, I guess, means taking all of her in: we can't spit out the parts we don't like. That is the lesson we are trying to teach her about life; the pupil is simply confronting the teacher with the lesson she's been taught.

The only person on the unit who connects to her all of the time is Philip, a new M.H.A. Philip and Fay are often seen huddled in a corner of the dayroom, their bodies very close together, knees and noses almost touching. Philip is a recent convert to a new belief system. I know very little about this system; I don't even know if it has a name. Here's what I know: its adherents wear ankle-length robes and wool caps. They use body oils, incense, and herbal medicines to safeguard and promote their connection to the eternal. They are vegetarians. Their mottos often contain foreign words about the need for peace in the universe and the soul. Philip and others who share in these beliefs move and speak slowly, smile often, and often look as if they know something you don't know and there's no way that they could tell you about it even if they wanted to, which they don't, because you just have to experience it. It's like The Religion of Be There or Be Square.

Although staff is pleased to see Fay choose human contact over solitude, there is something peculiar about Philip that no one likes. He's secretive, for example. One of the basic rules in the hospital is that any communication between a patient and staff or trainee cannot be private. If it is deemed significant, it needs to be documented by writing it into the patient's chart. Otherwise, patients can create division between colleagues; in addition, information is the coin of the realm and cannot be hoarded. Philip's problem is that he does not agree with this rule.

When Tom accuses Philip of withholding information about Fay by not writing into her chart after their conversations, he argues the point. He feels that he has a relationship with Fay that supercedes the hospital rule about information. He is very polite and agreeable, and even concedes that there is more than one way to look at the situation. Needless to say, he's out of a job by the end of the day.

It is time to conference the patient. I have done everything to help that I can, but Fay's course has been topsy-turvy. Her status is now what it was when she first entered the hospital. She is starving, reclusive, and psychotic. This woman has no beginning, middle, or end. Perhaps one of the meanings food has in her life is the definition it gives her with respect to time and space. Three times daily people talk to her about something they can understand together.

The consultant I choose to hear the case and give his opinion is Robin Archer, a staff psychologist. Robin is extremely self-assured, thin, beautifully dressed, and attractive. He is eloquent and outspoken about his patients and his practice with them. "I won't see someone as a private patient unless I like that person," he said once at a psychology department meeting. We were all shocked by the boldness and truth of the remark. It took us a long time to understand that Robin did not mean strictly a patient's immediate likability, but rather was implying the importance of respecting the individual's struggle and creativity and that person's efforts to integrate into a whole his confusing and painful experiences. Robin is the most empathic and least intellectualizing clinician in the department. He speaks plainly. If anyone can connect to Fay on her terms, it is Robin.

Before the conference takes place, Robin asks to meet with Fay on the in-patient unit. I accompany him. His behavior with Fay is more instructive and fascinating to observe here than it is in the conference room. For one thing, he is very gentle. He keeps his distance. He talks to her in soothing, sleepy tones, and closes his eyelids at times when she answers him. When he says the word "yes," he makes it into a polysyllabic vehicle, with emphasis on the final consonant so that the word positively snakes into the atmosphere. His words are not as important as the way he chooses to breathe life into them. It is not clear whether Fay appreciates this distinction, because her behavior during the interview with Robin isn't any different than the way she acts with me.

"She's one sick cookie," says Robin afterward as we descend the stairs from the locked unit to the day hospital where the conference is to be held. Then he pauses, and says slowly, the way I imagine the ex-M.H.A. Philip talked about the restorative powers of sunshine, or the color blue in the spirit world, or life after death, or whatever it was that he and Fay discussed in secret, "We have to allow her to be herself. And if that means regressing, becoming like a little girl again, then we have to give her the permission to do that." We take a few more steps. "She's so sad. She is so unbearably sad."

Fay remains in the hospital until the end of my internship year. Upon termination, the plan is to transfer her to a halfway house where her daily life can be supervised by a trained staff. Maxine and family would prefer her at home, but no one has the time to keep a constant eye on her, nor does anyone want to take the responsibility of making certain that she is always safe.

Very little has changed about Fay. We still regard her as a diagnostic mystery. She hasn't responded well to the medication, which is to say that she's still psychotic and depressed (although even more secretive about her feelings than at the beginning). She attends groups now and then, but usually stays in her room, staring into space. She won't talk willingly. When she speaks, it is to confide to others her peculiar set of beliefs. When she refuses to eat, we threaten her with liquid medication (intravenous fluids), and she complies quickly with our orders. I've thought about her, and thought about her, and thought about her—we all have—and I still don't know who she is or what she was trying to tell me about herself.

When I think of Fay's appetite, the words of Kafka's hunger artist, in the story *The Hunger Artist*, come to mind: ". . . I have to fast, I can't help it," says the hunger artist. ". . . Because I couldn't find the food I liked. If I had found it, believe me, I should have made no fuss and stuffed myself like you or anyone else."

THAT MAN

Spontaneity and trust are rare on the locked unit. Staff and trainees are usually aloof toward patients who, in the most natural way imaginable, behave sadly and fearfully. For example, an in-patient often can't remember, without a physical effort that others can see, an experience with a parent where he felt valued by either mother or father. To make things worse, in-patients are sometimes convinced that complete strangers, with whom they have little else in common, know the most intimate details about them, and that these people (a.k.a the staff and trainees) use that private knowledge to make decisions about their lives that they may disagree with but are powerless to prevent.

Who in their right mind would demand to be admitted as an in-patient to such a place? Most of the admissions to the locked unit are brought here *involuntarily*—by family, friends, or legal authorities—because they are judged to be homicidal, suicidal, or unable to take care of themselves due to a major mental illness. This isn't simply treatment. It is also containment. A rare individual is the one who comes to Comm. Mental asking to be locked up in a psych. unit because he feels that the wrong in his life can only be made right by getting help in a mental hospital.

Mr. d'Alvirs is that man!

I met him three months ago at Eastmark Clinic. He had come in off the street, red-faced and enraged, walked up to the receptionist's window, and pounded its ledge while shouting increasingly strangled demands to see a psychiatrist. He is a little man who throughout the tirade kept a tan coat folded neatly under his arm. Meticulous, I thought, and wondered, how come? He was told to take a seat beside other people waiting in the smoky and dirty lobby that is littered with ash and cigarette butts bent like accordions.

"OK," he said, and strode into that room taking crisp but uneven steps like a military man learning a drill. He sat down, crossed his knees, and jabbed his index finger at the receptionist. "Fine. But fuck you, OK? FUCK YOU! *FUCK YOU!*"

After he completed the necessary paperwork, Mr. d'Alvirs was assigned to a clinician for an intake interview. It was my turn to see the next walk-in patient. I went over to him and put out my hand, saying his name and introducing myself. He brushed right by me.

"Where the Hell are we meeting?"

"He won't bring me my two boxes of cigars. He agreed to meet me downtown, in front of the South Street train station, and when I went there, just like he told me to do, he didn't bother to bring the goddamn cigars. And he'd promised, and he didn't say he was sorry, and when I lost my temper he started saying that I won't ever get the cigars. Well, he's a fucking idiot! And now I'm so fucking mad that if I get the chance, POW! I'll kill him. I will."

It became apparent soon that Mr. d'Alvirs had a relationship with his father that was more complicated than most, even mine. Immediately, I was impressed by how freely he railed at the old man. It was positively liberating! Although he is middle-aged, I kept thinking of James Dean in *Rebel Without A Cause* when I looked at him. Mr. d'Alvirs's anger was the most impressive thing about him by far.

"I need to be in the hospital," he continues. "Got it? I need treatment. And I need to be kept away from my dad. I need to be locked up. Because I'm very upset and very dangerous. If I'm not put in the hospital, who knows what will happen or what I'll do? And if anything happens, you'll be responsible. So get going, Dr. Haas. I expect to be inside in less than an hour."

A cursory review with Mr. d'Alvirs of his history reveals that he has never behaved dangerously. While he waits in the examination room, threatening to explode, I phone father. He is a retired municipal judge. I want to check up on the facts, and I need to tell him about his son's threat. (The law states that confidentiality must be violated if the patient is a threat to self or others.)

The old man is not upset. In fact, he is mildly amused and even chuckles a bit between clearing his throat a lot. We are treading familiar ground for him. He talks to me as if we're old acquaintances who meet regularly at a gentlemen's club for drinks and cigars, without the wives, surrounded by other sets of old acquaintances pleased to be similarly unencumbered and showing it.

Harumph. "Paul's been a nuisance, let me see now, since, oh, about 1959." He clears his throat again. "I recommend that you tell him to return to his room at the boardinghouse at once or there will be no allowance this month." Father shushes my expression of concern about his safety. "Tell him I won't stand for any more of his threats. I mean it this time."

I discuss the case with the psychiatrist and the two residents who are also working on admissions that afternoon. They agree with father. How can I give son the news? He is not dangerous or frightening, he's ridiculous.

■　　■　　■　　■

"Mr. d'Alvirs, I spoke with your father, and he and I agree that you don't belong in the hospital. It sounds like you're feeling pretty angry right now. Maybe you ought to go back to your room until you cool off."

"And why don't you go fuck yourself?"

Before I can respond to the insult, he starts to count off reasons that he feels make it necessary for him to be in the hospital. He says that he might go out of control, and when I dispute this, he says that anything could set him off.

"I'm a time bomb," he said. "I could blow up in a second."

By the time we reach the end of his list of reasons, he is in tears. I feel awful. This man must be miserable if he wants so badly to be a mental patient.

I return to Dr. Kohl, the senior staff psychiatrist on admissions duty that day, to ask his permission to see Mr. d'Alvirs as an out-patient. Like most psychologists and psychiatrists, I am attracted to misery, and the struggle between son and father interests me more than just intellectually.

In his first three months of therapy, Mr. d'Alvirs talks mostly about father. Father is a good man, a kind man, "a pillar of the community," but he is also a brute. He never listened to son, he never took him seriously, he never showed him that he loved him. Although he is now almost fifty years old, the brutishness continues to amaze and preoccupy Paul to the degree that all of his other feelings of love, for others and for himself, must pass through that paternal filter.

He lives alone in a boardinghouse. He never married. He has no children. He doesn't mention friends. He is unemployed and last worked fifteen years ago as a janitor in a community center on the West Coast. He lives on social security checks and a monthly allowance father sends him.

He can only name a few activities that give him pleasure. He has a modest collection of recordings of Broadway musicals, and every night plays an album all the way through until the end of the show. He also sends a monthly donation of fifteen dollars to an orphaned girl in Ethiopia whose name and address he received after writing to a charitable Christian agency. Finally, he loves to masturbate—three, four, as much as five times in a night.

"If I had a girlfriend," he boasts, "I'd be great in bed."

Our therapy sessions contrast with his behavior when we first met. Who would have imagined then that someone so consumed by rage could also be this unhappy?

As therapy progresses, he talks more about his sadness. I hear less and less about how scary others have found him to be. It seems to me that he is beginning to find therapy useful. All that changes when he comes in, shaken up, teary, telling a story about how he found a boardinghouse mate dead in the kitchen of a stroke last night.

He has a feeling that the exact same thing is going to happen to him, and I can't talk him out of it.

"What if I die before I have a chance to work things out with dad?"

The question terrifies him. He pleads to be admitted to the locked unit.

James Wells, one of two second-year psychiatry residents working with Dr. Kohl that day, opposes the admission.

"A hospital is for people who are sick," he drawls, "not for people who just want a rest from the normal difficulties we all find in life. Everyone needs to get away once in awhile. Mr. d'Alvirs ought to take a vacation instead of trying to check in here. This is not a hotel. Did you tell him that? Because if you didn't, I will."

James intimidates me both because of his status as a *second-year* resident and because he has incredible confidence. He is a little young to be possessed by so much arrogance. I am afraid to counter his challenge. Dr. Kohl, however, protects me by pulling rank on James. He allows Mr. d'Alvirs to be admitted. I imagine he sides with me because he likes me more than he likes James. Dr. Kohl has four sons. Wherever I see dads, I seek their approval. This has got to stop. Why am I so afraid to speak up?

"Maybe you'll learn something from this guy, Scott," says Dr. Kohl.

Wells: "I doubt it."

After the necessary documents are signed, I lead Mr. d'Alvirs upstairs to the locked unit. As is required by policy, we are accompanied by a security guard. Mr. d'Alvirs is admitted, and the guard dismisses himself.

We sit in his new room for a few minutes. When I tell him that I have to leave now, he croons a whine, then hides his eyes with the backs of his hands to mask the inevitable tears.

"I guess you're aware that Paul has a long psych. history," Alice tells me later in the day. She has just completed a physical on the patient. "Did you know that?"

"No, I didn't."

"Well, maybe you ought to take the time to find out a little bit more about him. Now that you've had him brought in here."

"Are you saying that he shouldn't have been admitted?"

"Hey, look. If Fred Kohl agreed to let him in, then it's fine with me. Just get to know the patient. I mean, I can't believe you didn't know he'd been in psych. hospitals before I just told you. What did you two talk about in therapy? You need to get someone's history before you have them admitted."

At this point in our training, Alice's ability to take an adequate history of a patient is vastly superior to mine, but it is not unique among her medical colleagues. As I have learned painfully throughout the year, the psychiatry residents have already been trained in medical school and during their medical internships to be DOCTORS before they started to undergo this education that will make them psychiatrists. As such, they take better histories of people who come to them in distress. Clinical psychology teaches the importance of the therapeutic relationship between clinician and patient; psychiatry also teaches responsibility. Since a doctor is going to be responsible for trying to bring health to someone who is suffering, that doctor needs to know as much as possible of the facts in a person's life before treatment begins. The success of a treatment depends on knowing *what* is being treated, what the results from other treatments have been, when the disorder first appeared (and was diagnosed), and what its course has been.

Psychiatry's appreciation of the history of the patient deepens my understanding of the phenomenon of mental illness and keeps its appearance in a patient from appearing to be an isolated and startling event. Psychiatry also asks me to look at a person's physical health and not just his behavior. At its best, psychiatry moves away from psychological *assumptions* and toward a more comprehensive view of mental illness.

I learn that from his twentieth year on, Mr. d'Alvirs has been in at least six different private and public psychiatric hospitals, for periods of time that range between one month and a year. Each of the admissions was precipitated by expressions of rage toward father. The content of the rage is that dad is not doing enough for him. Diagnoses of son have varied, and include the following: schizophrenia (undifferentiated, chronic type), schizoid personality disorder, major depression. He has been prescribed, and has taken, antipsychotic and antidepressant medications, but the drugs have not helped to improve his behavior.

I meet with father to get more history about son. According to him, mother's death twenty-five years ago was the event that changed Paul's life. During his adolescence, she had been in and out of hospitals for treatment of the cancer that eventually killed her. Father has not remarried.

"Paul took it very hard," says father. He pauses, shifts his glance. "He takes after his mother when it comes to the Feelings Department."

Within a few days, the treatment team considers Paul to be sedate enough to come down to the day hospital. We expect him to fit right in at once, but instead he reacts to its relative normality (compared to where he spends his nights) by regaling and frightening the women patients with braggadocio. He talks about drinking as if he is the Errol Flynn of the bottle. His supposed interest in alcohol is news to me. He has never mentioned the subject in therapy sessions.

I overhear him talking by the dayroom, in a hallway never lit.

"Oh, yeah, I must drink a quart of bourbon every night. Why, when I was really down and out, you know, I would sneak into my dad's house, well, it's still my house, too, but, see, I don't live there, so I call it his. I could live there if I wanted, but I don't. Who needs someone else's rules? I like living on my own. I like the independence. Making my own rules, staying up as late as I like. Anyway, he bagged me once drinking some booze from his liquor cabinet—I know where he keeps the key—and tried to throw me out. Out of my own house! I drank the whole bottle, right then and there. Right in front of him. And he couldn't do a goddamn thing about it."

Paul rambles as he tells the story. What if he really is an alcoholic? Should his treatment focus on alcoholism rather than his rage and depression, which could be symptoms of alcohol abuse or dependency?

This sort of diagnostic thinking is what comes of being trained primarily by the psychiatrists at Comm. Mental. They teach us to think about the physical world, as well as the imaginary one; as a psychology graduate student and then an intern I have been limited up to now by a bias in my education that typically has eluded an analysis of physicality and its impact upon behavior. With time, however, I am learning how to think like a psychiatrist. I feel both lucky and foolish about the lessons. Lucky because my skills as a clinician are broadening as a result of them, foolish because I am supposed to be training to become a psychologist. Why can't we include in our graduate education, and here among our staff psychology supervisors, more consistent work on the importance of an individual's physical health? After all, the question of Mr. d'Alvirs's alcoholism must be answered before treatment with him can be said to begin. It needs to be ruled out as a disorder.

■   ■   ■   ■

Fortunately, Comm. Mental has as director of its psychiatry residency program Charles Hardwick, a world talent in psychiatry, who is just now completing for imminent publication the profession's first major study of alcoholism. Charles is always on the cutting edge. He has let everyone in the training programs know that he will lead conferences to discuss any patient whose psychiatric problems are seen to be or suspected to be related to that person's alcoholism.

Like most of the other interns and residents, I am always thinking up ways to get supervision of my work from the psychiatric elite of the hospital. The crux of the internship is good supervision. We may not have opportunities to learn from these experts again. Their clinical experience, acumen, and compassion are vast and place them at the top of their profession.

In addition to our mandatory supervision each week, we are free to seek out any other supervisory experiences. Mr. d'Alvirs presents me with an opportunity to be taught by Charles Hardwick. Carol, the social worker on the case, sets it all up. She is also very eager.

Almost all of the day hospital one staff and trainees show up to Charles's conference. He is lean and immaculate in a tan suit with cuffed trousers, and wears one of those dainty, inoffensive pastel ties the men have on in advertisements picturing happy couples in Bermuda. Eleanor, the chief psychiatry resident, introduces him, flustered and polite. Charles brings out clumsiness in others. We are intimidated by his intelligence and class.

For forty-five minutes, Charles summarizes the findings in his study about alcoholism. He discusses the disease's genetic component, its symptoms, its function in the development of personality, and professional psychiatry's historical neglect of the problem.

We are dazzled by the new information. Most of us, psychiatry residents and psychology interns, were educated traditionally. We are not used to understanding the role that alcohol can play in psychopathology. No one has explained to us its importance and its presence in our society as epidemic.

Charles continues, and now he talks about dual diagnoses (for example, an individual who is both schizophrenic and alcoholic), and the need for alcoholic detoxification of a patient *prior to any* therapy for other psychiatric problems. Charles believes in the patient's *reality*. He trained as a psychoanalyst at the prestigious and orthodox (Freudian) Boston Psychoanalytic Institute, and because he understands the role of the unconscious, he does not limit himself to an appreciation of it when seeking explanations of human behavior.

After Carol and I provide a history of Mr. d'Alvirs, Charles says, "I'm prepared to see the patient."

This is my signal to go and get him. I have explained to Mr. d'Alvirs every single detail of how the conference will work and offered assurance to him that his participation in it is completely voluntary. But he still strides in before me, wiry and furious. He won't say why he's mad. Charles rises and extends his hand while the patient glowers at the packed house.

"Mr. d'Alvirs? I'm pleased to meet you. I am Dr. Hardwick."

They shake hands and sit down.

"Why don't you tell me what this is about?" asks Paul. "I don't have all day, y'know. I have some very important groups to go to, ones I like, by the way, and that includes woodworking, which I like very much, and then I intend to start looking for a job. I have decided to support myself. I don't want Dad's money anymore. He can stuff it. I know it won't be easy, but I can do it if Carol and Dr. Haas help me." He takes out pages of the classified ads from *The Boston Globe*. He has folded them a quarter of their original size, and stuffed them neatly into a pants pocket. "I've even circled a couple of jobs that might be right for me."

"I see," says Charles. "Well, Mr. d'Alvirs, I wonder if you could tell us all a little bit about yourself."

With no warning at all, Mr. d'Alvirs stands up and throws the newspaper pages at George's feet.

"Oh, for Christ's sake," he says, "fuck you! Go fuck yourself! I'm not going to sit here and listen to any of *this* bullshit."

He storms to the door, and slams it when he exits back onto the day hospital.

No one has ever seen Charles so completely at a loss for words. Almost a minute goes by in silence. No one knows what to say or do. We shift uncomfortably in our seats. When Charles smiles, finally, and then starts to laugh merrily, we all start to laugh with him. What's so funny? Who knows? But Charles has said it's OK to laugh. What a relief!

"Well, he certainly showed us that there are other things on his mind! Still, I hope that the first part of my talk about alcoholism will be useful to his treatment, if indeed he has a problem with alcohol, and in the treatment of others who are observed to carry that diagnosis."

Meanwhile, Carol has arranged for us to get weekly supervision from Alex Ellman. The family meetings with Carol, Alex, son, and father are more successful than the conference hosted by Charles. The supervision is dynamic because it takes place as events unfold in the family. Alex encourages Carol and me to talk, and he jumps in to make a clarification or interpretation whenever he feels it's necessary.

The sessions take place in my office. In his dark suit, and with his formal bearing, father reminds me of Frank Morgan as the Wizard in the movie *The Wizard of Oz.* He keeps his distance from Paul. He is nothing more than polite. Has it always been this way between these two men? When I look at him, I expect to hear him echo the Wizard when he was exposed by Toto, Dorothy's dog: "Pay no attention to that man behind the curtain!" How long has father hidden his feelings beneath the robes of a judge?

As the sessions progress, Paul becomes less intimidated by father and more outspoken. He feels supported and emboldened by the presence of us, his treatment team. Dad comes alone. The focus of the family therapy shifts magically, and suddenly, when Paul tells father during one of the early sessions that he does not "feel loved by him."

"I never felt that I meant much to you, Dad," he continues.

Whether it is through displays of anger or sadness, Paul flusters people with honesty.

"I . . . I never, I never, knew that, Paul. Uh. Uh. Of course, I love you. I thought that was understood."

"Well, I didn't know that, Dad."

We are all proud of Paul for speaking up. Our efforts in the family therapy are showing results. Alex compliments Carol and me on our work.

I open another front in the attack upon Paul's maladaptive behavior by getting a psychopharm. consult. So far he has not been medicated. Don Hibbert, the consult. service's chief resident, goes over Paul's history with me. He also observes the patient on the locked unit. Don is especially intrigued by two facts: Paul's spontaneous rage that does not seem connected to any real or immediate events in his life, and the possibility of underlying depression. He suggests a trial of lithium, a medication once heralded as a miracle drug for treatment of manic-depressive illness, the mood disorder characterized typically by violent shifts of rage and misery alternating with grandiosity, hyper-religiosity, and mania. This disorder, said to be due to a chemical imbalance, is treatable with lithium, which restores the balance. Lithium is also, at this time, starting to be used with people whose moods swing violently and without clear precipitants. Along with family, group, and individual therapies, a trial of the drug with Mr. d'Alvirs seems to both Don and me to be a great idea.

For once, things are fitting into place. Mr. d'Alvirs agrees to try the lithium, and it works. Which is to say that in a few weeks he is calmer and in greater control of himself. Although he is still essentially a loner, he approaches men and women on the day hospital to sit and chat for awhile. He stops talking altogether about his drinking prowess. He occasionally speaks up at the community meetings. He becomes more active. He looks happier.

And in his therapy sessions, he talks manfully about his loves and losses. For example, he mourns the death of his mother. He speaks of his dissatisfaction with masturbation and voices instead a need for "a real woman who'll love me." He is not guided completely by past events.

Somehow I have made the hospital work for Mr. d'Alvirs. He will never be quite anonymous, like the rest of us, which is to say that he will not fit into society as it is constructed, but clearly he now derives more pleasure from his circumstances and is better able to make changes in his life that will lead to greater satisfaction.

How did it happen? Why is his case so different from the others?

There are many reasons for the success. For one thing, I find it easy to imagine being in his predicament. And because my empathy is deep and immediate, I put more effort into the therapy with him. I also like his bravado. He is so scared inside, so weak, but damned if he doesn't try and show the world his toughness. His rage is like the judge's robes worn by his father. It hides his truest feelings, the ones that anchor him to life. He wants respect, and I can respect him. He has also responded well to a trial of medication. His destructive behavior and rage are made less intense by the lithium. Finally, unlike so many of my patients, and the in-patient population in general, Mr. d'Alvirs *asked* to be here. He wasn't brought in kicking and screaming like John Plummer, or handcuffed like Eddie Anastasi, or bewildered like Fay Shepard—he fought to get in. He demanded treatment.

But despite its success with Mr. d'Alvirs, I am still not at home in the locked unit. Not because the place is frightening or bizarre, which it is, but rather because it is unjust. With rare exception, Mr. d'Alvirs being *that man,* most of the patients have been placed there against their will. I understand intellectually why this has to be so: if released, they might hurt themselves or others due to a major mental illness. But emotionally, as I listen to their stories of bottomless rage and sorrow, I cannot help but feel that there must be a better way to help them.

As it is practiced in this country psychiatry does not agree that there is a better way. No alternatives exist to the locked unit for committed patients; there is little formal research funded or conducted that seeks to find one.

The psychiatry residents I train with justify the strictures of the locked unit endlessly.

"Would you want Anastasi running around on the streets?" John Kantrowitz asks. "Sometimes people are in need of treatment even though they don't know it. That's where being a doctor helps, Scott. We recognize that people don't always understand when they're sick. Somebody has to take responsibility for them."

"It's been a difficult year for you, hasn't it?" adds Jim, another one of the first-year psychiatry residents on the day hospital. He is a stout, constricted Minnesotan by upbringing, but his interest in psychiatry as both patient and clinician has made him unusually empathic throughout the year. "You're like a fish out of water."

All year I tried to be like one of the psychiatrists. I parroted them. They are the ones in absolute authority within a psychiatric hospital. And if you want to succeed in their world it means having to be like them. They want to see someone recognizable when they look at me.

But although there is a tremendous amount about the psychiatric model that I admire and seek to integrate genuinely into my work with patients, the process of integration ought to be a matter of choice rather than one of necessity. Because having to mimic psychiatry also means remaining uncritical of some things about it that are wrong—for example, the standard practice of locking people up in order to protect them from acting suicidal or homicidal, or from being unable to take care of themselves, due to mental illness.

Is there another way of making people less miserable?

It is not until the internship ends that I am able to ask myself this most fundamental question.

SUPERVISION

THE MOST IMPORTANT GROUP I BELONG TO

All happy families are like one another; each unhappy family is unhappy in its own way.
> —Tolstoy, the opening sentence of *Anna Karenina*

The most important group I belong to during the training year is the Saul Gold Group. Comprised of all the first-year trainees—eight psychiatry residents and six psychology interns—we are to meet for an hour once weekly, for the year's duration, with Saul Gold. We are told that Saul is a senior psychiatrist who completed training to become a psychoanalyst at the Boston Psychoanalytic Institute. That is all we know about him.

From the beginning (and after it ends), each of us has different ideas about the group's purpose in being, and who Saul Gold is. I imagine, for example, that this group will be similar to the others in which I have been a participant: either didactic like a small class at college, or oppressive like a family gathering where people intrude on one another's privacy. I am not looking forward to being here, because I feel certain that I will be overwhelmed and will suffer; and yet I wouldn't miss it for the world, because I hate to be excluded. For the past few years, Jeremy has attended six-week-long summer group seminars on body movement as a key to happiness; touching and massage to release tension; clowning, juggling, and dance as freedom from intellect, et cetera; and so he assumes that the group can in some way be like those earlier experiences: liberating. Jim, Judith, and Charlotte have all been in group therapy, so they think that perhaps this will be a therapy group.

Despite these and other widely varying perceptions, our group feels and tolerates enough love and hatred in common to elect to continue to meet with Saul, for a very small fee (two hundred dollars per person annually), when the training year is over, first at the hospital and then, at his home in Brookline for once-weekly sessions at 7:30 A.M. In what we suspect is the twenty-year history of the Saul Gold Group at Comm. Mental (it is practically an institution, a catechism of the place, but no one I ask knows precisely when it began), this has never happened before us. We meet for three years.

In early August, the first meeting of the Saul Gold Group takes place in the hospital's library for its patients. The room is cluttered, dark, and unclean. Most of the books in it are yellowing paperbacks, and most of them are scattered on couches, window ledges, and shelving. Floor-length curtains block light from barred windows, and we have to squint at first to see one another. By the time Saul steps in, chairs have been gathered by the group to form a circle with a gap that anticipates him. Suddenly, there is silence. We place new appointment books at our feet. We're here to listen, not to take notes, that much is clear, but no one knows what to say or do, we haven't been told yet.

The sight of him surprises me. He is almost completely bald, middle- to old-aged, thick-waisted, medium height. He wears pants that ride high up on his waist, has on mocha-colored, rounded shoes, and keeps his shirt unbuttoned at the collar. His face is hidden partially by eyeglass frames. Due to the informality, the unpretentiousness, he looks nothing like any of the other senior staff.

All summer I have listened to staff psychiatrists and psychologists, and second- and third-year psychiatry residents, relate myths and anecdotes about the great importance to them of the Saul Gold Group when they were in it during their training. As a result, I expect to see someone who looks like a Superman. And in this particular vision, I am traditional, conservative, one of the crowd; I imagined that Saul would look like the Marlboro Man. Instead, he looks like a *mensch*, a guy with no *chomas* (translation: pretensions). He could be someone in my family, a distant relation I greet exclusively at weddings, or at a bar or bat mitzvah, who asks me how I'm doing in school, and how nice it must be to follow in my father's footsteps, and whether I've thought about going into practice with my dad in New Jersey after my training is done.

This expectant vision and the extreme disappointment that never fails to follow it are essential to the ritualistic way I internalize and imagine clinical supervisors during the internship. So is the surprise that happens regularly each time. I also expect the supervisor to understand my feelings intuitively, and at once, and to be there to take care of me. When this does not happen (it almost never does), I feel abandoned and then enraged, entitled to something that is withheld from me because of that person's selfishness. I am ruled, in part, by this distortion, and it isolates me terribly.

Being in Saul's group increases my awareness of these feelings. That's partly why I hate and belittle the group immediately and imagine that I will feel like a failure and outsider in it. (One fails group by being silent in it, an observer rather than a participant.) I'm at the point in my training and in my life where I try to pretend that unpleasant feelings will go away if I ignore them, and supervision is a place where that pretense is confronted.

The silence is interrupted by a question from Katherine.

She wants to know if we will be meeting during August, when most of the other staff psychiatrists are away on a month's holiday. He tells us that we are free to get together in his absence, but that, no, he won't be here. Jeremy asks about the purpose of the group, and he answers: we are expected to show up on time and "to act spontaneously, but appropriately." Each week one person will be asked to make notes, at home, about that session (to be read to the group the following week).

Other questions follow. Each has its focus: Are we a psychotherapy group? Saul never answers directly, but his hints seem to me to add up to a sense that our group's purpose in being is to provide us with a forum where we can talk and listen to one another's feelings and thoughts as they relate to the intensity of the training, rather than that we undergo psychotherapy together.

"I don't see why you're all so eager to turn this into group psychotherapy," he says. "What would you gain from that?"

"Support," says Jim. "A chance to explore our feelings. More depth to the discussions."

"Why do those things feel necessary to you here?"

"Well, isn't that the purpose of the group? To support one another professionally? So that we see that we're not alone with the problems we have with our patients?"

"Ask the group."

Jim turns to us: "Why can't this be a therapy group?"

"Because," answers Roger, "some of us don't want it to be one."

"Right," agrees Graham. "I wouldn't feel comfortable undergoing therapy with my colleagues."

"But Jim," says Judith, trying to take care of him a little bit, "can't we support one another without this turning into therapy?"

"I don't think it will be enough," he answers. "But then it never feels like enough to me." He looks like a boy alone on a playground all of a sudden, so preoccupied in play that he hasn't heard the recess bell sound. "I'm never satisfied."

"Why not?" she asks.

And so Jim begins to tell the group about his adolescence,

the bitter struggles with his mother, and the protracted death of his father due to heart disease and diabetes. He cries toward the end, and a few of us shift forward in our seats as if to motion that we want to get up and hold him. Others, like Roger and Graham, look uncomfortably toward the door. To some, the group provides therapy; to others, it is a place to exercise intellectually. Saul never chooses sides; he sits still and doesn't say a word.

Throughout our time together, the unanswered question—What is the Saul Gold Group?—serves as ballast to our discussions. Some want the group to provide psychotherapy, others threaten to drop out if that happens, and a few contend that it already has happened. Saul insists that a psychotherapy group differs from what we're doing together, but he is not specific enough about the differences. He is extremely vague.

Outside of this room, we are a group that is used to having our questions answered. As a result, many of us become irritated by Saul's "withholding behavior." The term comes from psychobabble, and translates into English as "If you, Saul, loved us, the group, you would answer our questions. You choose not to answer in order to punish us." It is easier to call Saul withholding than to say "You don't love me." Psychobabble creates a lexicon without feelings. Saul knows this; he wants to stir things up, to make us react rather than contemplate and create distance.

It's not easy to make a group of shrinks lose their cool, but he does it. It is one of his unstated goals. He compels us to question what lies beneath the surface of clinical neutrality. He does this by refusing to answer our questions.

For example, Jim, exasperated, between huge grins and chuckling, asks, finally, "Why do we have to come here? And why won't you tell us what the group's supposed to be about?"

"Why not ask the group?" asks Saul.

"Aren't you the group's leader?"

"I think that every group has to have a leader."

"Well, what are we doing here? I know that the group is

supposed to contribute to our training, but how? Are we supposed to come here each week and gripe? Or are there specific things you have to teach us?''

Saul laughs merrily in response, and Jim becomes visibly annoyed.

''I don't see what's so funny,'' he says. ''I don't understand why you won't answer my questions. If you ask me a question, I have to answer it. Don't the same rules apply to you?''

''Why is it so important for you to have me answer your questions? Why do you need to know that?''

It's an uncomfortable situation for all of us to be in, and we're glad that Jim has appointed himself interrogator. He holds that appointment until the very end. It is how he wants to relate to Saul, and how we want to relate to him. At the same time, Saul won't answer Jim's questions, so why does Jim keep asking them? And why do we allow it?

Maybe he gets pleasure from the Socratic exchange. He certainly revels in it. He is center stage. Saul will not budge. His unwillingness to move preserves and perpetuates his relationship to Jim, and by extension, to the group. It's like a father-son magic act in a second-rate nightclub, or the vaudeville routine between Harpo and Groucho Marx.

As they perform, we become an audience for the Saul and Jim Show, which is safer than participating in it.

From the outset, Saul cultivates the mystery one necessarily feels when sitting in a circle of chairs with an older stranger. Trained in psychoanalysis, and a true devotee of its principles, he believes as much in silence as he does in words. We are not clearly directed toward stated goals, and any structure that develops to the group will be a factor of our needs and desires, many of them rooted in earlier experiences, successes, and failures we cannot forget or remember.

Saul is an old-timer, apparently, not overly impressed by the new biochemical, genetic, or technocratic explanations of the soul. He avoids the vogue terms, used frequently by the younger staff psychiatrists and psychologists, when describing patients: object relations theory, chemical imbalance, affective disorder, an Axis I diagnosis in *DSM-III-R*. He talks instead about how people act or imagine, and his words are simple and convincing. (Step One of my ritual: in order for me to belittle the supervisor, I must first idealize him.) At Beth Israel, where he teaches in the psychiatric residency program, Saul is known as "he who speaks English."

Unlike most of my other supervisors, he uses earthy parable or confusing aphorism to confront our desires. For example, later in the year when Jo Ellen, one of the psychiatry residents, expresses anger toward the group for what she feels is its insensitivity toward her, Saul listens, and then remarks: "When you can't fuck, you fight." It is his pithy, vulgar, provocative way of saying that a person is enraged when unloved. Naturally, Jo Ellen becomes apoplectic in order to prove him wrong—or to prove him right.

This is a scary group to be in. There's a sense I have that you never know what will happen next. It's sort of like life in that way—another thing I'm afraid of most of the time during the internship. Growing up in a household where the Holocaust was as real as sunlight, I am almost as familiar with death as I am with the living. Lord knows, I don't want to talk about these peculiar ideas in this group (or almost anywhere else). So most of the time I endeavor to keep my mouth shut.

Acknowledging my true feelings, to say nothing of expressing them, is most difficult for me during my training. I am alone most of the year, in and out of romantic relationships, or purely sexual ones, but never attached to anyone for very long (except imaginatively, to my ex-girlfriend, who isn't attached to me), and I idealize and then belittle myself as I idealize and belittle others. For example, I think that I am great and original, or I think that I am a complete failure. There is very little moderation in the views I have of myself. And rather than confront these distortions, I appoint myself to be a man silenced or amused by his anxiety, just as Jim appoints himself to be interrogator, in the group.

During its first session, for example, I can't wait for the group to end. I wonder what it would be like to have my true feelings exposed to the group, and then I remember how I felt as a child: anxious and isolated. I don't like being this way, I feel sad all of a sudden, and when the session ends finally, I am relieved, glad to rush off to the psychology department so as not to miss a moment of what is almost certain to be another of its interminably boring weekly meetings.

Saul returns after Labor Day. He's tanned and well rested. There are many rumors about where he's been. I've heard people say that he has a house on the Cape, in either Truro or Wellfleet, both exclusive communities packed with psychiatrists every August. Someone else said he goes to Stockbridge in the Berkshires. Or has he been to Israel? Naturally, no one asks, because by now, after the one meeting with him, we have learned that not only doesn't he answer your question, but he tries to engage you in dialogue to determine why it is you've asked in the first place. He is convinced that a question is as revelatory as its answer. He also believes that most questions are answered best with a question. These are two of the ways in which he cultivates his mystique.

By remaining a mystery to the group, Saul confronts us with the truth that his identity, as we perceive it, is a composite of how we relate to him, and that those junctures are a repetition of earlier relationships that preoccupy us. Being in the Saul Gold Group is like being in a family. Although it is not nearly as powerful as that, the pressure to increase awareness of my feelings and thoughts about Saul, myself, and the others reminds me of that experience.

At the same time, the whole thing is a little bit weird. I barely know these people, and I'm not about to begin talking about my feelings with them. For one thing, I'm miserable and anxious. And I'm not sure that I want them to hear me admit what some (who are my friends) know and many suspect to be true. So for the time being, I make lots of jokes, engage in antics, or keep my mouth shut.

Through my involvement in the group, I come to realize that talking instead of feeling, using humor, and being silent were all ways I behaved in my family when I felt sad or afraid in their company.

While he was away, we all tried to gather information about Saul from the second- and third-year residents and the staff. A second-year resident told Roger that Saul is the son of a rabbi. Alice heard that he went to Yale Medical School. Yesterday, Jim saw a woman driving a car with vanity plates that read "SAUL GOLD," and now he asks Saul if she is his wife.

Sheepishly, almost as if it is expected of him, and that he would prefer to answer rather than dodge it, Saul dodges the question: "What made you assume it was my car?"

"The SAUL GOLD vanity plates," responds Jim dryly, but with the eagerness of a smart kid showing off by quickly spelling difficult words correctly in front of a grammar school auditorium filled with kids from all the classes, kindergarten through fifth grade. We perch on our seats because it looks as if Jim is on the edge of getting a straight answer.

After a big more dodging, a few more questions to questions, Saul admits that the driver of the car with SAUL GOLD vanity plates is his wife.

"All right!" says Jim, and then he claps his hands together and laughs triumphantly as if he has just witnessed a physical contest, a sport perhaps. "You did it! You actually answered a question!"

We all laugh, even Saul joins in, but I feel disappointment, too. I can't understand what the fuss is about. Jim's question and Saul's answer seem to me to be beside the point. So what if he's married? And driving a car with vanity plates! That seems to me an empty boast, trivial, lacking worldliness.

From the beginning, each of us in the Saul Gold Group holds and fulfills the requirements of a different self-appointment. As Jim interrogates, I belittle. Not that we are limited strictly by these posts; but rather, we each act certain ways in the group most of the time according to how we see (or desire to see) ourselves in it. These visions are primarily a product of earlier experiences that have nothing, ostensibly, to do with the group.

For example, I believe that I tend to belittle Saul because, in part, I feel overwhelmed by his importance. Growing up with a father who was snatched from death by *luck alone,* I find that my love for another human being is always overshadowed by the imagined or real loss of that cherished individual. The constant threat of loss leads me to idealize and then belittle, dramatically, out of proportion to reality, the importance of that human being. It's like a lifelong rehearsal for the actual event.

Naturally, this systematic outlook has some basis in truth, both that of my own past and that which we can all agree is the actual, and the result is that it complicates completely how I imagine others and myself, and how I become intimate.

Others in the group also hold appointments. John Kantrowitz, a psychiatry resident, behaves cautiously and intellectually, and guards himself from engagement by using technical terms rather than simple ones. For example, instead of saying that he feels strongly about something that is said in the group, he says, "I have a lot of strong affect about that." This way of behaving is attractive and facile due its superficiality; an appearance of involvement is created when very little is taking place spontaneously, without calculation. Several group members adhere to this approach in varying degrees: Graham, Roger, Charlotte, Nick, Vincent, Mary, and Linda. They measure the weight of their words before allowing others to judge them.

Then there are the group members who speak emotionally about their lives. They feel a freedom to do this, I imagine, because many of them are in individual psychotherapy, an experience that aims to halt the self-imposed regime, the exile into the Self, the ritual that has as its purpose repetition. They are outspoken about the pleasure and misery in their lives. In this group I think of Jeremy, Alice, Judith, Meg, Simone, and Jo Ellen.

Although I feel that I don't belong to either subgroup, I'm probably more like one of the judges than one of the accused, a surprising turn of events for me to have to consider because I like to think of myself as open and insightful. But during the internship, I'm rigid most of the time, or scared about being rigid or rigid about being scared, or amused about being scared of being rigid.

I also tend to obsess about extraneous details rather than meditate on my true feelings. And when I discover something unlikable about myself, I pretend to feel differently or try to make a joke about it. For example, when someone sees that I am uncomfortable in the group and asks me if I am uncomfortable, I am likely to say, in a high-pitched, unnatural tone, "No! No, not at all. No, I'm just tired. No." Or when I am asked about my anxiety and how I feel it interferes with my ability to work as an intern, I try to make everybody laugh: "Completely," I say. "It interferes completely." And then I hope that, satisfied by the meager joke, they will leave me alone. I want to get rid of these feelings I have. They surprise and frighten me, and I prefer the uneasy division between intellect and emotion to that. I am insufficiently curious about who I am, and like instead to imagine and pretend who I ought to be.

Late in the second year, an incident occurs that typifies how we function as a group with our varying appointments. Somehow the question is put to all of us: Why did you choose to become a psychologist or a psychiatrist? Saul suggests we answer in turn—one of the rare times when he makes a suggestion of any kind, so we do as we're told. We are excited, and feel safer, having been provided with structure.

But when my colleagues start to talk about why they went into the professions, I find the answers to be too neat and too shady: unremarkable, predictable, patented for an audience. They say, "I wanted to combine my love of medicine with my interest in people," or "I've always been the sort of person people find it easy to talk to," or "It's a profession where you can combine various disciplines, like philosophy," or "I was the one in my family who did most of the listening." This last response seems closest to the mark, but to me it still falls short of being true. In addition, I want to stir things up in the group, to provoke people away from their calculated and aloof positions, so I say, knowing that my statement will be seen as inappropriate, "As a child I always wanted to know what was going on in my house behind the locked bedrooms and locked bathroom door. So I figured as a psychologist I would find out."

Predictably, there's cool intellectual silence and disapproval. Ironically, it's what I'm looking for. Now, in the middle of the second year of the group's meeting, too much has gone on for it to appeal to me any longer. By now I want out. Not as part of my tendency to belittle supervisors; I have stopped performing that ritual through work in psychotherapy. More important, I have moved in with Laura, a family physician I met a year ago. As a result of this relationship, I feel more alive and expressive, and have even less need to talk to people in the group about my concerns.

Finally, although certain ugly quarrels are going on between several people outside of sessions, the issues that intensify and prolong these fights are rarely brought into the group. The group conspires to keep silent about problems it doesn't want to deal with, and gradually, as is the case in a lot of families, more isn't talked about than is talked about. We become converts to the ancient and pervasive belief that silence is the best remedy for pain.

So why do I keep attending group sessions? Why not quit? After all, Linda, Roger, Judith, and Jo Ellen have dropped out for varying reasons. But I stay until the bitter end.

I stick around because, in part, I'm always the last one to know when a relationship is over. I am also afraid that I'm going to miss something. But miss what? Goodies? There are no goodies.

Depleted and preoccupied by both these concerns, my participation in the group becomes increasingly superficial. For example, this is how my notes read about one week's session:

> Last week much talk surfaced around intimacy, competition, and endings. These experiences cover much of life

in general, so to be more specific—some of the residents spoke briefly about conflicts having to do with interviewing for the same job. Charlotte, Katherine, and Simone spoke of mixed feelings about research they plan to do next year. Many spoke of losses they had suffered. And it seemed that throughout our time together, closeness and regrets surfaced. I find myself wishing that the group could continue for another year. It has been a place where I have started to learn more actively about my own and others' sense of weakness and strength that's completely different from any other place I've been. And while it doesn't always feel safe here—it is intimate and there is usually a struggle to be honest.

As for these notes—I thought about them a lot all week. They took too long to write and it was painful and I went through many processes and wrote many drafts. This didn't happen the last time I took notes. I wish often that we could just be colleagues, accepting and sharing differing values—and this has been something the group has taught me over the years. It's like: What lies beyond competition? At times this group has given me a sense of what *is* beyond that.

Wow, what hokum! My notes have nothing to do with how I am truly feeling or thinking. They are vague. And they have an external focus, a self-consciousness that is manifest as seeing myself as I imagine the group sees me, and how I would like to be seen by the group.

Most importantly, I never mention in the notes that I don't want to be in the group any more. Instead, I say the opposite. No one questions this disparity (which must be obvious to someone other than myself), no one confronts me about the overly intellectual, unfeeling, false qualities of my notes. The silence is a typical reaction to anyone's reading of their notes in the group, and it comes about because all notes are acceptable as long as they have as their focus the group itself. Hokum is fine as long as it is hokum about *us*. The group loves to hold a mirror up to itself and admire its reflection.

This is one of the main reasons our group continues for three years. It provides a place where the exaggerated degree of one's self-importance is never confronted. Despite the great frequency and intensity of the doubts and the complaints about our work and ourselves, we believe that we're really something special, an elite, a cut above the rest. The Saul Gold Group never confronts this arrogance, which is an explicit part of our training at a Harvard Medical School hospital. This group, instead, is a place where all of our "spontaneous and appropriate" feelings and thoughts are acceptable most of the time. If we are arrogant, that's OK. That's how we feel, right? And all feelings, as long as they are "spontaneous and appropriate" are important and equal.

What good can come of this?

Saul accepts us. When an intern or resident begins to cry, for example, while trying to talk calmly about a difficult parent, or about the loss of a relationship, or about a failure at work, or about the shame that must accompany confession, he listens without making judgment. He does not interrupt. He helps us in these ways to identify and then care about the imaginings of ourselves that we are ashamed of.

We try to learn to listen like him. He listens like Theodore Reik, psychoanalyst and author of *The Third Ear,* whose humor and childlike amazement informed his ability to remain interested in people like an artist, not to classify or even to try and cure, but rather to understand and in this process come to love them precisely for their contradictions and suffering. Saul's acceptance is like an embrace.

Being accepted in the group inspires new thoughts and feelings about my work. I can more easily tolerate mistakes I make, and confusion I feel. I also take the acceptance I feel in the Saul Gold Group and apply it to other situations.

For example, I begin to have greater compassion for my family. I imagine the groups that they have been in, and are a part of now, and how these groups shape their real and imaginative lives. They feel unloved, at times, an experience rooted in the truth of their histories. For my father, it was facing the unmitigated wrath against the Jews in the place of his birth; for my mother, it was a series of familial mishaps, none extreme, but many tainted with unkindness and even cruelty.

It becomes easier to love my patients, because, like all children, I grew up loving people whose histories also hold experiences that injured them and made them feel unloved. Because they are familiar, I am drawn to those who suffer.

I care more about the mentally ill than those who trust only in reality, because I feel that somehow they do a lot of our suffering for us. They suffer like the so-called identified patient in a family. The identified patient is the one who is hospitalized for treatment of psychosis, for example, but who comes from a family that is abusive and peculiar. The family believes that the patient is the problem, and that if he could only straighten out then things would be dandy. The mentally ill seem to me to be the identified patients in our society, in our culture, and I am drawn to them because they are the most outcast, the most misunderstood, the most unfairly treated, the most unloved. In the family of humanity, which is the most important group I belong to all of the time, it is the mentally ill who need the most acceptance and love.

Learning this lesson is the main purpose of the Saul Gold Group for me, and why I stay in it for the three years. Although there are extreme differences between us, we all have interest in and love for our patients. We also have struggled since the beginning to offer to one another feelings of support for the difficulties we share in clinical work with the mentally ill.

But despite its success, the group's value diminishes over time. Being accepted and supported in it means that little of our behavior is interpreted. After all, we are not a therapy group. We are a group of psychology interns and psychiatric residents joined together by . . . by what? By our sense of self-importance? By the conviction that our concerns are paramount? By our work?

As the group's time together draws toward a close, I recede more into silence, and into my own thoughts. I can't leave the group, but I'm not engaged in it either. I enjoy being accepted, but it isn't enough. I want confrontation, but I refuse to bring it about. I want out, but I won't leave. The situation is static, but I won't change it.

Instead, I sit with the others in a circle of plush furniture in Saul's living room overlooking a pond and the trolley that is forever clattering by, and join the intellectual talk about our importance as clinicians. Magazines about travel, economic policy, the Soviet threat, and psychoanalytic theory lie in stacks on a circular table beside a long gold couch. Paintings hang on the walls. A pair of large, framed photographs of children are propped on a piano top.

By now I imagine that everyone is also a little tired of the group, and that they, too, can't leave it for reasons they will never talk about. The group ends, finally, when the third and last year of the psychiatry residents comes to a close: many of them are leaving town. A core of about ten of us will remain, but for reasons that are never fully discussed, we don't elect to continue.

"What else would you want to get out of the group?" Saul asks those of us staying in the Boston area.

No one can provide a good enough reason for continuing, so we all agree to stop.

As a gift to the group, just before it ends, Katherine has printed an expensive booklet that contains our names, addresses, phone numbers, and the names of our "significant others." We ooh and ahh over its cost and design—she's obviously put a lot of effort and thought into its appearance—and then put them away. These directories provide a good metaphor for the group: inclusiveness based on exclusivity, a roster that contains the facts about us but none of the feelings.

When the Saul Gold Group ends, we never meet collectively again. Afterward, I feel a great sense of relief: I wish I had been honest enough with myself to leave earlier.

WHAT DOES IT MEAN
TO BE LATE
FOR SUPERVISION?

JANUARY

Mr. Plummer and I sit side by side on a couch in one of the noisy dayrooms on the locked unit. Mental patients surround us, repeating themselves through gesture and words and songs. The TV is blaring a commercial for a Chevy Camaro. Although we have not yet said a word, it feels right somehow to be together like this. Both of us have struggled to be close all year, and to sit next to one another without comment is an achievement. We don't need words to explain ourselves. The acceptance comes from the proximate act.

When two people who are intimate sit in silence, a union can be assumed, a degree of comfort, a refuge. We trust each other. For Mr. Plummer, the feeling of safety accompanying this act must be atavistic or new. I enjoy his company, while most people he contacts in life avoid him. Either they don't see through his strangeness, or they are afraid to identify with the boy who is cowering beneath that surface. He feels alone most of the time. And his solitude is not monkish, but rather like that of a prisoner who has been placed in solitary confinement because his presence in the community is judged to be too dangerous, or because he is undesirable. Why? What is it about his grief and madness, his visceral longing, that unsettles those with the power to judge him?

The acceptance we share, however, is a pleasure. After our battles over medication have ended, and after my anxieties about how to cure him have been quelled, being able to sit with Mr. Plummer is a great relief. I no longer want to cure him. First and finally, I want to accept him. And it looks as if that is possible this morning. Although he stares straight ahead, wordlessly, and fails in any way to acknowledge me, I know that we have lowered some barrier between us. He doesn't get up and walk away. Nor do I. Unlike the others, I welcome him.

Naturally, I lose track of the time because I am enjoying myself. And I don't wear a watch. (I last wore one in the fourth grade. I looked at it constantly. I became obsessed with knowing the time. Now I figure it's better not to have one rather than to drive myself crazy that way.) So it isn't until Christina walks by that I know, by turning her wrist toward me and seeing the small, round face of her Timex, that it is 11:10.

Suddenly I feel a tightening in my chest and a shortness of breath. I realize with alarm that I am going to be late to supervision for the first time. I am rarely late for anything. I stand up, drop my appointment book and some folders, scattering everything pell-mell in the process, and look up at Mr. Plummer who hasn't moved at all. As I gather up my stuff, I say to him: "Mr. Plummer, I'm sorry, but I've got to go now. I'm late for another appointment. I'll have to see you tomorrow." He makes no response at first, but then he says, "I'm sorry to see you go."

The remark feels like a personal triumph. I can't wait to talk it over with my supervisor. What might it portend? Are we connecting at last?

From my position on the floor, I watch Mr. Plummer rise

and walk to his room. His posture is perfect. It is painful to watch him go. I rise, too.

The path to supervision takes me two flights up through unlit stairwells. I climb two steps at a time. I hate being late. It also feels like exercise to dash up the stairs. I remember reading in his diaries or letters that Kafka ran up and down stairs as a form of exercise. (It's typical of him to have chosen a redundancy, a passageway toward or away from people rather than the human contact itself.) It is his very lifelessness that appeals to me. I am out of breath.

When I reach the fifth floor, I cross through several dark and unoccupied rooms where the occupational therapists conduct their workshops for patients. Scattered about on the long tables are scraps of cloth and newspaper, the remnants of papier mâché dolls or the occasional collage. Little tins that once contained frozen orange juice concentrate now hold scissors, crayons, pens, and pencils. There is glue and there are scissors to put things together or to take them apart to form other shapes. Guided by the therapists, the patients make small products that can then be sold downstairs in the hospital's gift shop or kept by them as souvenirs of a hospitalization.

Next I pass by the patient's library, also the site of the Saul Gold Group. I peek in. A volunteer functions as librarian. She stands behind the small desk, and as I watch she pulls a beaded brass cord to become illuminated by a bulb.

Turning right at the end of this long corridor, I see several makeshift offices used by first- and second-year psychiatry residents. Their plaster-board walls are thin. I hear a patient yelling at Graham, a first-year resident on day hospital two: "You're too fucking passive! You just sit there. I want you to help me, and you just pretend to listen! You need to get more involved!" After a pause, Graham says, "You have to see things from my point of view! You're never satisfied. And I'm getting sick and tired of your accusations!"

In the final stairwell between the set of offices and my destination, I come across a lump of a human being who sits on some steps. Upon closer examination, I see that it is an old woman with gray hair. She looks up at me, grimaces, and then makes a chuckling, chortling, choking sound like an animal that has caught its foot in a steel trap and sees no way out other than to gnaw off the offending appendage. This is the moment before she sinks in her teeth.

And now I'm in the psychology department. The door to my supervisor's office is open. It is 11:15. Our appointment was for 11 o'clock. I step in.

"Robert. Hi. Sorry I'm late."

He looks up at me. At once, he narrows his eyelids. He doesn't ask me to sit down. He doesn't say a word. He taps a pencil onto an even stack of papers atop the desk. The sound made by the eraser is dull and ominous and slow. Tap. Tap. Tap. Tap. Tap. Tap. I think of dirges I've heard in movies or on the TV. I sit down. My experience with psychiatrists and psychologists informs me that an inquiry into my being late is about to begin. For some reason, mental health professionals hate tardiness more than other people. I have a terrible feeling that I am about to find out why this is so.

Robert looks especially annoyed and aggressive about having been kept waiting. I've had a tough morning, and I don't know if I can handle an investigation into my behavior right now. You never know where it will lead. When shrinks get mad, all the *mishegas* beneath that calm surface explodes in a million different directions. He still has not said a word. Maybe he will let me off the hook if I change the subject. He stops tapping when I ask, "Where should I start?"

I place a manila folder between us. In it are the results of psychological testing with Howie, who is one of Judith's patients.

"I'd like to talk about this Rorschach," I add with false cheer, still hoping that he can be persuaded to set aside his feelings. He does not flinch. Now he looks at me with curiosity and rage. His incredulous expression suggests that he finds it hard to believe that I don't share his need to discuss my lateness.

So much between shrinks goes on through mind-reading stunts. After all, who knows what he is really thinking? He hasn't told me yet. "Or, if you'd rather, I'd love to talk about Mr. Plummer. I think we're making progress in our therapy."

At last, Robert ends my small talk.

"Before we do anything else," he says, robbing the words of warmth, making each of them into little hammers, "we need to talk about why you're late to supervision."

"Robert, I'm sorry. I ran late in my session with Mr. Plummer on the locked unit."

"Weren't you aware of the time?"

"I don't wear a watch."

"Maybe you ought to get one."

"Maybe."

"Are you trying to be clever?"

"No. I just don't see what concern it is of yours if I. . . ."

He cuts me short.

"So how did you learn what time it was?"

"Christina walked by. She had on a watch. When I found out it was ten after eleven, I ran over here."

"Why didn't you ask someone for the time earlier?"

"I didn't think it was late."

"What made you think it was late when you finally did ask?"

"I don't know, I just did."

"No idea?"

"No."

"You've never been late before."

"I know."

"So this time there has to be a reason. What's your reason?"

"I just told you the reason."

He brushes it aside.

"That is not satisfactory. I need to know what's going on."

"What *is* going on?"

"Think about it."

In my head, I hear a police sergeant on TV say, "Book him."

Silence among the psychologists and psychiatrists at Comm. Mental is a way of life. Robert stares at me. He weakens my resolve. I will have to deal with this, after all. But I don't know how to placate him. Perhaps the way out lies in trying to guess what he wants to hear and then saying it. Can I find a clue in my knowledge of Robert?

Robert Hamilton is a staff clinical psychologist. He supervises one of my therapy cases and most of my diagnostic psychological testing. He is lean, angular, dark. He is in his late thirties, a wunderkind in the community and nationally known for longitudinal research on individual psychoanalytic psychotherapy with people who carry the diagnosis of borderline personality disorder.

He is hip, too.

For example, he talks excitedly about Broadway plays he's seen recently, dines at out-of-the-way ethnic restaurants ("Man, you should have tasted the Lat Thoke Soong I had at Mandalay last night! Sizzlin'! The best I've ever eaten!"), and cooks Cajun at home. His wife is also *au courant*, an architectural historian whose expertise lies in Edwardian furnishings.

I know all this about Robert because he talks about himself and his interests as introduction to our supervisory sessions. I enjoy listening to him because there is something attractive about a man who has outlived his circumstances. Robert has reinvented himself. It gives me hope that I can do the same. I often feel that I would also like to be someone else other than who I am.

"Scott, what is going on?"

"I told you already. I can't think of anything more to say about it. I'm sorry I'm late."

"When you are late," he says, "you devalue me and the supervision."

"I'm sorry. That wasn't my intention."

"What was your intention?"

"I didn't have one. I lost track of the time."

"I don't believe in accidents, Scott."

I sigh and look out the window.

"Am I boring you?" He pounds the desk, and papers fly, and I bounce back and blink. I remember suddenly an incident with Mr. Leo MacDougall, my history and Latin teacher for the sixth through the eighth grades, who lost his temper whenever he caught one of us not paying attention in class. At first, his rage was absolutely terrifying, but after a while it became a game to provoke him so we could skip the day's lesson. I remember Leo's last tantrum: it was directed at me because I could not conjugate the verb *amo*. He got so excited and confused by his feelings that he slammed his wrist down on the desk and later that day it swelled up and turned black. He broke blood vessels. "Do you think what I'm saying now is unimportant?"

"What?" I'm still thinking of Mr. MacDougall. "No. No, I didn't say that."

"Then why did you just sigh and look away?"

"Because I don't know what else to say to you. I'm sorry I'm late. I told you why I was late."

"What is going on?"

"Excuse me?"

"What is going on?" Robert does not like to repeat himself. He is one of the rare psychologists to have been permitted to attend the prestigious Beispeil Psychoanalytic Society in New York—traditionally a bastion limited strictly to physicians—and due, in part, to his training there, he must see repetition as a sign of weakness or of madness rather than a facet of the human condition, like having a heartbeat.

He hates the feeling of not being taken seriously. By now he's practically yelling at me. "You don't wear a watch, you're late for our supervision, you don't seem to care, and you're annoyed because I want to understand why you behave this way."

"Sorry."

" 'Sorry'? That's it? You're sorry?"

"Right. I'm sorry I was late. Hey, look, if I knew you were going to get this annoyed I would never have been late."

"Well, that's a start." He snorts. "That's the first thing you've said all morning to show me that you understand and can appreciate how I feel."

Although the intensity of our fight is extraordinary, the arena where it takes place is not. During the internship supervisors hold all the power. Some are more willing to share it than others, but control belongs to them.

Each week in the hospital all interns and residents have at least eight hours of individual clinical supervision of their work with the mentally ill. The supervisory relationship itself often becomes a topic for analysis in the supervision. If this seems solipsistic, it is. The boundaries of what is acceptable in discussions include much more than what is ordinarily OK for people to talk about. Supervision at Comm. Mental is different from therapy in that it does not provide treatment; it is similar to therapy in that it aims, through confrontation or interpretation, to identify areas where the supervisee's thoughts and feelings interfere with, or intersect with, the psychotherapy that individual is being taught to provide to patients.

For example, when I appeared anxious and preoccupied with Peter Mendelsohn, another one of my supervisors at Comm. Mental, he suggested, somewhat delicately, and with embarrassment, that I begin therapy. When I asked to talk things over with him, he said, "No, this is supervision, and we can't have that kind of relationship."

When I appeared to be the same way with Peggy, she also suggested that I get into therapy. "You seem to be afraid of your feelings," she said gently, "and when you feel that way it must be difficult to tolerate the strong affect of your patients, many of whom are very sick." She pointed out to me a problem that *I* was bringing into the therapy session with my patients. She did not want to rid me of the difficulty herself.

Typically, supervisors do not analyze or try to reform behaviors or feelings or thoughts; rather, they may suggest that the supervisee take up with a psychotherapist the problems that have been identified in the supervision.

So what Robert is doing is really quite different. He not only wants to increase my awareness of what he sees as problematic, he also wants to talk things over. Maybe even do a little therapy, who knows? The more I think about what he's doing, though, the angrier I get. It feels humiliating to have to put up with his inquiry, and to be unable to say, simply, "It's none of your business. I'm late. I'm sorry I'm late. I won't be late again. OK?" But I don't yell back at him because I am afraid that he could create plenty of problems for me during an already difficult and painful internship.

What am I supposed to do?

"What did you expect would happen when you showed up late?"

"I didn't think about it, Robert."

"But you did know you were going to be late, right?"

"Right."

"How do you feel about being late now?"

"Badly."

"Go on."

If I knew what he was looking for, I would say it. The truth is that I've had enough, that I feel badly about being interrogated, not about being late. But since I still don't know the magic words I must eventually have to say, I elaborate upon my initial excuse.

"I suppose I could have gotten here faster. As soon as I found out what time it was, I panicked and dropped all my books. And en route to your office, I was distracted by things I saw along the way."

"You say you 'panicked'?"

He pronounces the word delicately, the way a detective might lift a scrap of evidence in a gloved hand.

"That's right."

"Any other thoughts?"

"No."

"No?"

"No."

He looks at me as if from a great distance, as if the answer is right there in front of me if only I would open my eyes and see it. But again: who knows what he is really thinking? We are engaged in mind-reading here. After all, we are both working with assumptions that neither of us has made explicit.

Until, at last, Robert makes his thoughts known to me.

"I think I know why you're late," he says, after a long pause. "I think I know what it means when you're late for supervision."

"Oh?" At this point, I am eager to hear what he has to say. He has badgered me for over thirty minutes, and I am exhausted. At least the police allow you one phone call. Here I am, though, under arrest for no reason at all, unable to contact an advocate.

Before Robert can say a word, I bet with myself that he will say that he's hurt because he enjoys talking to me at the outset of the supervisory sessions, and that because I am late, the message I have communicated to him is that he is not an interesting person.

"Maybe you're late," he says, with finality, "because it's too hot in here. You know what I mean? You know what I'm talking about?"

"No."

"Perhaps you're sexually attracted to me. And that unconsciously you decided to show up late in order not to have to deal with your sexual feelings for me. Maybe these feelings make you uncomfortable. Because when you're late, you spend less time with me. It is less intense that way."

"You've got to be kidding."

"No, I am not joking. And I want you to think about it."

I don't know how to respond to the accusation. Most of all, I feel embarrassed. He feels elevated by his pronouncement. He is incredibly powerful suddenly, a man with real X-ray vision.

Only it doesn't seem true. I don't have these feelings for Robert. I mean, sure, he's cute and funny and attractive, but so are a lot of men and women I meet. It doesn't mean I want to go to bed with them. For God's sake, I came to supervision late, had hoped to discuss my session with Mr. Plummer, or the results of psychological testing with Howie, and discover instead that my supervisor wants me to meditate on my sexuality.

After waiting awhile in an effort to convince him that I've given the matter the most careful thought possible, I say, "Robert, I don't think so. I really don't."

"You don't? Are you sure?"

"I'm sure."

"I want you to think some more about what I've said to you."

"I already have. I know what I'm talking about."

I think immediately about an intellectual crush I had on Ernesto Marquez, my literature professor while I was an undergraduate at Hampshire College. My fantasies about him were not sexual, but were rather ones in which I felt safeguarded. I was impressed by his certainty, and his dogma, because I had so little to anchor my impressions at that time in my life. I looked forward to our meetings and always showed up early because I wanted to be near him.

The sanctuary he provided me in our talks about the literature of the Third World continues to guide my intellectual growth. Especially important were his efforts to teach me to understand the subjective psychology of people—their consciousness, their literature, their choices—whose experiences are completely different in all ways from mine. When I am with Mr. Plummer I often think about Ernesto, and I try to give him that same support. I want to talk to Robert about all of this, but his rage makes that impossible.

"I am being honest. I am not sexually attracted to you."

He looks crestfallen. Is homosexuality a theme from the psychoanalysis in which he is the patient? Is it something his psychoanalyst *accused* him of the last time *he* was late to one of *his* sessions? I am irritated by having to guess how he is feeling, by having to wonder how to placate him, but it is clear that I will never get out of here otherwise.

"OK," he says. He is not so noisy now. In the homophobic

psychoanalytic community, homosexuality is considered a per-
version and an abnormality. According to their traditions and
terminology, a homosexual man fears castration so much that he
chooses another man as a partner to avoid having to bed down
with a woman, who he imagines is a castrated human being.

I do not exaggerate. In a chapter entitled "Perversions and
Impulse Neuroses," the psychoanalyst Otto Fenichel, writing in
his classic text *The Psychoanalytic Theory of Neuroses,* states,
"The recognition of the fact that there are actually human beings
without a penis leads to the conclusion that one might also become such a being; such an observation lends effectiveness to
old threats of castration. . . . Homosexual men react by refusing
to have anything to do with such frightening sights thereafter."

Because I have not regressed or become defensive in response to his accusation of being castrated, Robert decides that
it must be time to take up a new strategy: empathy. He will kill
me with kindness. Now he's the good cop. He smiles! His posture relaxes.

"What is it then? Why were you late?"

I have an inspiration. I will tell him the story of my life this
year. I begin, and soon he knows almost everything. He listens
carefully, does not interrupt, and offers support and concern at
all the right passages.

"You mean you and your girlfriend broke up a month before the internship started?"

"That's right."

"Wow. That must have been awful. How long had you two
been together?"

"Four or five years, depending on who you talk to, me or
her."

"It felt like a long time."

"Right."

"Had you lived together?"

"Yes, for a year."

Oddly, I am not aware of being annoyed by his intrusiveness. I am that out of touch with my true feelings, that eager to
please. I'm glad to see him happy. I'm more concerned about

his well-being than my own. That's what power does to me. I want to honor the judge even when his opinion goes against me. I am that enthralled and frightened by power. If Robert is aware of this peculiar attitude, he doesn't mention it. After all, he is for the moment its beneficiary.

After we talk about my past relationship, Robert wants to know about the women I've seen this year. I tell him about Christina, and about most of the others. He nods his head sagely. In sum, Robert is delighted by my confession. His smile is beatific. He also looks as if he has received a blessing of some sort.

"So you were late to supervision because you're anxious," he says, joyfully. "And because you and your girlfriend ended your relationship, you've had a pretty difficult year. Am I right?"

"You're right."

"So isn't it important for you to share that with me? In order to keep from acting out the anxiety by being late again?"

I am about to say that I was late because I don't wear a watch, and lost track of the time, and ran over in my session with Mr. Plummer, but I decide not to spoil things. We have made progress, after all. He is happy, and although I am still under arrest, the charges against me may eventually be dropped.

"You're right, Robert," I say. "You're absolutely right."

Just before today's supervision ends, I make a few jokes about how being from the New York area, I'm not used to people being so uptight. I say that people in Boston don't talk about their feelings the way I'm used to talking about my feelings back home near The City, and that I'm glad to have had this opportunity now. He laughs at the reference to New York, pleased to recognize it, and to know what it means. (He is originally from Maine.) It's like we're both hip, man.

Meanwhile, I am thrilled to be out of there. I feel insulted and degraded, intruded upon and misunderstood. Because I am only an intern, I don't discuss the incident with any of Robert's colleagues in the department. I figure that they will take his side. And I vow never to be late again.

■   ■   ■   ■

The next morning I am back beside Mr. Plummer on one of the lumpy couches in a dayroom of the locked unit. In this graceless world we inhabit, the suffering we know is no longer stark or separate. To one another, we are not the prisoners of others' imaginings of us. I do not view him as mad. He does not question my sexuality, the most vital of human experiences. As Ernesto taught me during our long conversations on literary theory and the language of the Third World, we must begin to try and imagine the subjective psychological experiences of others when it is impossible to see ourselves in them. I think that this is what Mr. Plummer and I do for each other today.

We look forward to getting together, even if it means not saying a word. Our time together is a refuge from cold theory. He gestures, I gesture back; two solitary prisoners tap out a code on the bars of their cells, knowing that there is no way to escape, but enjoying, for the moment, the music of their communication.

THE WALK-IN CLINIC/
EMERGENCY ROOM

Every Friday, my routine changes completely. I am assigned to Eastmark, Comm. Mental's walk-in clinic and emergency room. People are hauled in unwillingly by police or in an ambulance, or they come to us on their own, without a fixed appointment, to be evaluated for treatment. They are suffering or disorganized, or someone thinks that they are out of control (dangerous due to their mental illness) and that because of this they don't belong among us. Many of these patients have not been previously diagnosed, which means that it becomes our responsibility to determine the causes of their pain and how it can best be taken away or lessened.

Our options for treatment usually vary: admission to the locked in-patient unit; assignment to a day hospital; acceptance as an out-patient; prescription by a psychiatrist of antipsychotic medication and a follow-up appointment to determine the efficacy of the drug; transfer to another facility (for detoxification of substance dependency, for example); or being turned away if seen to be malingering.

151

To malinger means to fake the symptoms of a mental illness in order to be treated like a mental patient. Why someone would want this assignment, I don't know, but it happens often enough that an individual walks in complaining of hearing voices (also known as auditory hallucinations), for example, and during the diagnostic interview is found to be discontent, but healthy enough in most other respects. Typically, just like the mentally ill whose behavior they mimic, these people have no one else to turn to: no family, no friends, no co-workers, no acquaintances in the neighborhood. They are homeless or living alone, unemployed or underemployed, and without the hope that their situation will change. And so they tour the city's psychiatric emergency rooms, asking to be taken in and made a part of something larger than themselves. By pretending to be mentally ill, they hope to join the only club that will admit them as a member.

The malingerers and the mentally ill I meet at Eastmark share the intensity that comes from being alone in the world. Embracing their feelings makes me aware of my own loneliness. When I am able to imagine their suffering, and their dignity in the face of it, I feel hounded, too, and disliked, and cut off from society's enterprise. I think that's why the Them and Us mentality prevails in the mental health professions. By cutting Them off, we create the illusion that They are not at all like Us, and that We do not harbor the thoughts and feelings that They embody.

If we view madness on a continuum, however, we have to become aware of those features of our souls that we would rather pretend do not exist. The constant shuttle of patients through Eastmark confronts the commotion inside the clinician who observes as if from a distance. But in the end, there is no faraway pain, and there is nothing remote about their suffering. In many ways, *They* are just like *Us*. Their misery and their madness are fundamentally human experiences.

I believe that's an important part of why the mentally ill are quarantined; to know that They are simply more vulnerable to the horrors of existence is intolerable because it means that the horrors, whether real or imagined, are familiar, and that it is the reactions to them that vary most. The mentally ill realize this better than any of Us. So We separate Them in order not to be reminded of what We all know to be true: that the world is unsafe, unpredictable in how its cruelties are meted out, indiscriminate about its choice of victims. There is no right and wrong. There is no foundation, no canon of normalcy. Through no fault of their own, children and adolescents emerge as adults having experienced horrors within their families and within their societies and, as a result, they become the mentally ill I meet at Eastmark.

When we find ourselves alone in the consultation room, my first feeling is fear because I am face to face with someone other people want no part of. I see a human being whose individuality is hard to believe in or to define. So much of it has been erased by experiences in which that person was made to feel worthless. They show up wearing hand-me-downs or clothing from Goodwill Industries or the Salvation Army. The people who come to Eastmark are at the very lowest points in their lives, during what is often the worst crisis imaginable for them. Pain has robbed them of the capacity to improvise; they are often unable to tell me what's wrong in their lives, what specifically has brought them to this point of having to talk to a complete stranger about that which horrifies or saddens them.

To complicate the relationships formed at Eastmark, the people who come for help often expect me to behave toward them like an old and dear friend. I get knowing winks, or stares full of fury, and when I ask what's wrong, I am told, slyly, "You know," as if I know. But I don't know! How could I know? I'm not a mind reader. We've never even met before.

"You a psychologist?" asked a gnomelike man who walked in with complaints that red, white, and blue bugs planted in his teeth by the CIA and FBI were devouring his nasal passages and making it impossible for him to breathe.

"That's right."

"Read my mind!" he shouted gleefully.

My protests make no difference. People continue to imagine that I know their deepest secrets. When I insist that I don't know anything about them, their hope changes to rage and terror. Suddenly, they are convinced that I am lying, and that I will humiliate them by revealing their secret to everyone. Or, that they don't deserve to hear the truth. Either way, they feel invalidated. And they're used to being lied to so much that they don't believe me when I continue to deny what they suspect to be true. They've heard *that* before!

They often expect me to be able to know their feelings without their having described them, or to tell them what to do, or how to live their lives. But mostly I am in awe of their resilience and their ability to survive. If I had to live with their pain, it would certainly kill me.

My first task is to overcome my fear. Their suffering orients them. Their compass is pain. Overwhelmed, they are unable to contain or to understand their feelings adequately. As a result, their demons fill a room, haunting those closest to them.

Despite the discomfort I feel in facing them, I try not to be like others they have known: judgmental, hateful, undependable, quick to violate, self-absorbed, a real betrayer of the trust that makes relationships possible. My efforts often make no difference. They respond toward me as if I am monstrous, anyway. They project onto me their past experiences, and I am defined by them before I can prove that I'm any different.

Naturally, this complicates the diagnostic interview further. But I try to let them be who they are, and they try to allow me to get close enough to get the necessary information. After all, if I can tolerate their projections rather than react, I can learn a little bit about what is going on inside them. And if we're fortunate enough, I can even be of help.

I usually have no more than sixty minutes to diagnose—to determine what is wrong—and then to recommend treatment. There are almost always others in the waiting room who need to be evaluated.

Immediately following the initial intake/diagnostic interview, the case is presented to Fred Kohl, the senior staff psychiatrist who supervises the walk-in clinic every Friday. He is also assigned to supervise the clinical work of James Wells and Zoe Jaeger, second-year psychiatry residents. The four of us discuss the patient.

Following our discussion, Fred interviews the patient while we observe. Afterward, we discuss the patient again while that person sits in the waiting room. The final step in the intake process occurs when the initial interviewer—James, Zoe, or me, depending on the rotation—informs the patient of the team's decision regarding his treatment.

Fred Kohl is in his mid sixties. He has a shock of white hair and a bushy moustache. Sprockets of hair pop out of his ears. He looks athletic. He acts tough. For example, he is gruff, impolite, and profane. He talks about hard drinking, promiscuity, and World War Two. He is always reading a paperback detective book or a spy thriller that he carries around in an otherwise empty briefcase. Occasionally, he reads favorite passages to us from a John Le Carré novel. He drives a sleek, foreign black sports car with M.D. plates. He continues to smoke filterless Camel cigarettes even though just about everyone who knows him in the hospital has begged him to quit. The sound of his hoarseness, the rasping, can be heard two doors down. He also suffers from angina, which was just diagnosed last year. Fred is not well, but he won't admit it readily.

Instead of talking about his health problems, Fred constantly regales us with terrific stories about the past, from his days as a bomber pilot during the world war. It is easy to imagine him striding into officers' barracks on an air force base near London, or roughhousing in a pub, or flying low over the shattered patchwork that was Germany, sighting targets, seeing people dash for cover, letting loose the bombs over Berlin.

Fred remains direct about what to do with enemies, which these days are feelings that as a cluster comprise what we call mental illness. He wants to stay in control. If only he can stay in control, the world won't be so complicated and frightening. Maybe death won't find him. If he doesn't think about it, it becomes less real. He still engages in the denial he feels is necessary to solve problems. Fred's response to fear is to pretend that it is someone else's problem we are talking about.

Fred acts as if he believes strongly in the Them and Us mentality. He is the expert. He sees what is wrong. He tries to fix it. Despite this conviction, however, he never compels supervisees to be just like him. That compulsion is the main flaw of the supervisory process. Fred understands this. With him we are, within reason, free to work as we like, to develop our own clinical styles, and to make our own mistakes (as long as there is no possibility of harm coming to the patient). He is the one with the thirty-plus years of experience, but if we want to do things differently, it's OK—as long as the job gets done right. He has told us that he believes that there is more than one way to try and help someone in pain.

Fred's tolerance and encouragement of diversity is unusual at Comm. Mental. The hospital is filled with experts who believe that the best teachers develop informal schools of theory and practice in which their pupils learn to think like them. Fred's experience has taught him otherwise. He just wants to get out of here alive.

Toward the end of the day, he sometimes gets quiet and shares meditations about death with us. He is sad about how old he has become, and that his body won't obey him. But he won't make the changes that might increase his years. He feels that it is too late for that. Besides, it would be an admission of weakness, and who knows where that could end?

So instead he talks ruefully, with humor and nostalgia, about "the cards life has dealt" him. Then he says: "Time for a drink." Fred's toughness is superficial. Beneath the surface, he is afraid. His willingness to let us know this about him is an important lesson of the supervision. It enables me to accept my fear of what comes next. He teaches not from the textbook alone, but also through the strength of his character.

A man walks in with a baseball cap. A pair of college police, just past their teen years, in ill-fitting, freshly pressed uniforms looped with ringed walkie-talkie cords, drop him off. They found him wandering the campus, talking to himself, invoking deities and bugging students, who are a little testier than usual since this is the week of finals. He looks down at his sneakered feet when I address him by name, which is Mr. Dobbs.

"Mr. Dobbs, what brings you here?"

"The police brought me here."

That's a pretty concrete response. Doesn't he know where he is? This is a mental hospital, not the Bureau of Missing Persons. Most walk-in patients at least know that.

"Yes, right, but why do you suppose they did that?"

"A case of mistaken identity," he says without feeling. He sits rigidly. He looks to be about sixty. "They think I'm someone else. But I'm not the man they think I am."

"Who do they think you are?"

"Better ask them."

"And who are you?"

"My name is Calvin Dobbs. I live in North Cambridge with my big brother. You can call him to see that I'm telling you the truth. His name is Alvin."

Alvin and Calvin, give me a break. Mr. and Mrs. Dobbs didn't have much imagination. And nor does their son, it appears.

"It sounds like you want to go home."

"*Yes, I am.* I don't want to be here. And I would appreciate it if you would please let me leave as soon as possible."

"OK."

He stands up.

"May I go now?"

"Not yet."

He sits down again. I look at him. He looks at the floor and then at the walls. Is he preoccupied?

"Mr. Dobbs, do you hear voices?"

"Shh!" He bends down his neck, squints, and cups his left ear with his left hand. After a few seconds go by, he says, "No. Do you?"

I look at the pink commitment paper the police brought

with him. (He has already been evaluated briefly by a psychiatrist at the student health services, who filled out this form re-
questing that he be committed to a locked in-patient unit for a
ten-day observation period.) I read that Mr. Dobbs was "shouting about God and the devil warring for his soul."

"Mr. Dobbs, are you a religious man?"

"A religious man."

"They say you were talking about God. Can you tell me
some of your thoughts about that?"

"Thoughts about God."

"Right. What are your thoughts about God?"

"Thoughts about God," he repeats. I'm trying to determine
if he has any religious delusions, or whether he is hyper-
religious, but he won't cooperate. Is he holding back information?

"Are we finished? I'd like to go home now."

"Soon, soon. I have a few more questions I'd like you to
try and answer for me."

His tendency to be concrete makes questioning difficult. Is
he limited intellectually? We often admit to the in-patient unit
mentally retarded adults who have decompensated and become
psychotic under the stress of frightening experiences. When they
become upset by something and don't understand how the world
works, their uncertainty increases to the point that they no longer
know what is real and what they have imagined.

"Mr. Dobbs, who is the President of the United States?"

He stares at me. It looks like he's trying to read my lips.
He shrugs.

"Can you tell me the year?"

Again, he looks at my lips. This time he says, "I haven't
had a beer since last night."

Has he been drinking? He doesn't look or smell drunk. He
wears a pair of tan corduroy pants and a short-sleeved shirt that
is too tight. He smells of apple juice.

"Mr. Dobbs, how much do you drink each day?"

"Couple of beers. No hard stuff."

The rule is to double the intake and doubt a denial if there's any suspicion of alcohol abuse that hasn't been put to rest. But I still don't know if this is what's wrong with Mr. Dobbs.

"How are you feeling?"

"I feel fine," he says. His smile is thin, pink, wan, an afterthought rather than an expression of sentiment.

"Yes, OK, but what are you feeling? Sad? Happy? Angry? What is it you're feeling right now?"

"Tired. I'm tired."

"What time did you wake up this morning?"

"Bacon and eggs. Sometimes ham and eggs. Depends."

"And what time did you go to sleep last night?"

"I kept the window open and now I have a slight chill. It must have gotten below fifty last night. That's what they said on the radio this morning, anyhow."

Mr. Dobbs doesn't understand what I'm saying, but why? I can't diagnose him because he can't answer my questions.

"Mr. Dobbs, will you excuse me for a few minutes?"

"Certainly," he says. "Do you know when I'll be leaving?"

"Soon, I hope, soon."

"Thank you very much."

After I present the case to the walk-in team, Fred interviews Mr. Dobbs. He receives the same confused responses until he asks about the service. After learning that the man is a World War Two veteran, he talks war with him, something he enjoys doing with any patient he meets with a military record. Mr. Dobbs claims that he was in the Third Army; he says that he crossed the Ardennes, that he was in infantry, but then got switched to communications corps. He performed sabotage behind enemy lines, he says, was caught, imprisoned briefly as a P.O.W. near Cologne, and then rejoined Patton's forces on their march east.

"He's definitely not a 'tard," says Fred, the moment the door is shut behind Mr. Dobbs. He waits outside for our decision.

"A *what?*" asks Zoe.

"A 'tard," he repeats. "You know, a guy that's mentally retarded."

"Oh, Fred," she says. "Honestly. That's a slur. Come on. Really. Can't you use the proper term?"

"No, it ain't. They're 'tards as far as I'm concerned. I don't go for this 'developmentally disabled' shit. I call 'em 'tards because that's how people treat 'em and that's how they feel about themselves."

James looks menacingly at him. Fred likes to say dumb things that he knows will upset people. He doesn't believe the prejudices, but it gives him the opportunity to prove that he's not so old that he can't still get a rise out of people. Because Fred *is* old.

James says, "I'd like to interview the patient. If you don't mind."

"I don't mind."

James takes Fred's seat. Fred sits between Zoe and me, looking boyish all of a sudden, his elbows balanced awkwardly on the arms of the chair, the striped blue pants of his seersucker suit riding up to his calves.

"I want you to count up to one hundred by sevens," says James. "Like this: seven, fourteen, twenty-one. . . . Go ahead."

Mr. Dobbs stares back at him.

"Seven, fourteen, twenty-one," he begins. And then he stops abruptly.

"Go on," says James.

"Seven, fourteen, twenty-one."

"Now tell me what this proverb means: 'Strike while the iron is hot.' "

"I'm quite comfortable."

"And this proverb, what does this one mean? 'One swallow doesn't make a summer.' "

"Well, swimming, deep sea fishing off of Georges Bank when I get the chance, walking to Harvard Square. That sort of thing."

"Thank you very much, Mr. Dobbs." James stands. He motions Mr. Dobbs up.

"May I go home now?"

"Not yet. I will be right with you. I want you to wait outside for me in the waiting room. I will come there and talk to you soon. I can help you."

He leads him out by an elbow, indicates to him where he should sit, and returns to us.

"He does not understand what you say to him," says James. "He confabulates answers. Sometimes he can guess correctly. He is good at faking it. And he fakes it the entire time. He is not making conversation."

"How come?"

"He may have Korsakoff's," James explains in scholarly tones. He is the most pedantic psychiatry resident in the hospital, but his pedantry is rooted in a genuine love of facts, all facts, the whole assortment. He's not showing off; this is how he sees the world, as an assembly of truths people shy away from. He is not afraid to be outspoken. He loves to speak in a precise clip. "This disease is caused by alcoholism. Due to his heavy drinking, he has developed a thiamine deficiency. He has receptive aphasia—Wernicke's disease. Which means he does not understand what people say to him. Let's try and treat that. Let's get him a massive amount of thiamine and see what happens. If his memory improves, we've caught it early enough to make the difference. If not, he has Korsakoff's, which is irreversible. But I do not think that is the case. He's in good shape. If he had Korsakoff's we would expect to see greater deterioration of his personal habits and hygiene."

"How can you be so sure about this?"

"Experience." He chortles with self-effacement. "And knowledge. Remember, I'm a *second*-year resident!"

James's certainty impresses me so much that I decide to talk to him about a problem that has been bothering me all year. We arrange to meet near the end of the day during a break between patients. He is in his tiny office, which is reached by going down a series of labyrinthine corridors in the basement. Along the way I pass below parallel rows of heating and plumbing pipes that are painted the same sulphur color as the walls and ceiling. The linoleum floor is filthy. I don't understand why James would choose to work in this part of the hospital until I reach the door of his office. In contrast to the rest of the building, here it is silent. I can hear myself think, and the voices of patients and staff seem distant. I walk in.

James is writing in a notebook at his desk. He stops and motions me to a seat. He closes the book. He stares at me.

"What is it? When you said you wanted to talk to me, I assumed from your tone that it was important."

"It's about my dad."

"What about him?"

"Well, he's a psychologist, too, and the thing is that when I do this work I can't help comparing myself to him. This upsets me, but I can't seem to stop. When I do things the way I think he would do them, or act the way I've seen him act, I feel second-rate, a cheap imitation. But when I do things differently, I feel incompetent or like a fraud."

I expect James to meander with the subject, to get as caught up in the confusion I feel when considering it, or at least to offer some empathy, but instead he narrows his eyelids and says coolly, "He had his chance."

I immediately feel sadness and relief. James's response seems exactly right to me. But instead of thinking about it, I start to talk again, to try and distract us both from the other responsibilities of growing up that are part of considering my dad in the past tense, as no longer the only heroic ideal.

"Right, James, right, OK, sure, but when I'm successful with a patient I feel like I'm betraying my dad somehow, like I'm letting him down by not acknowledging that he is the only one who can solve problems. It's like this: whenever I do a good job, like diagnosing someone correctly, or getting a person involved in therapy, I feel like fucking up just so my dad can step in, rescue me, and take care of me. I think that without him taking care of me, I'll be alone in the world. I mean, *he'll* be alone."

"Him or you?"

"Him, him."

"That's not your problem. Too bad for him."

James sounds as angry as I'd like to be if I was brave enough. Instead, I am sad, confused, and afraid. I expect to be punished for my thoughts. I imagine my dad walking into the office, interrupting our conversation, and pulling me up by my shirt collar to drag me home again.

"Yeah, but I feel a sense of responsibility toward him."

James is silent. At this point, I want him to behave toward me like my dad. I want him to tell me the right way to solve this problem. I want him to tell me to be just like him. But James won't do it. He looks back at me with curiosity, in the way that we look at the walk-in patients.

"And then there's the guilt. I feel guilty when I achieve success. Sometimes I even hold back on behaving competently because of it. It's as if my growing up as a clinician means the diminishment of his powers and his abilities. As if there exists a limited amount of strength in the world, and the stronger I become the weaker he gets."

"He had his chance," he repeats, adding, "and now it's your turn. You have to choose."

"Between?"

"Between fucking up and not fucking up."

When I return upstairs to Eastmark, Fred hands me an intake form. I'm next on the rotation. I find my patient and bring her to the consultation room.

A middle-aged woman walks in and takes a seat. She wears a man's navy blue raincoat that she has put on over a flannel nightgown. A kerchief partially hides a huge, sixties-style afro that is no longer fashionable. She's living in the past. How come?

"Ms. Harmon, what brings you to the hospital?"

She clasps her hands and places them in her lap. Her movements are stiff and awkward. I don't see any feelings in her face.

It looks as if she has stood before a mirror and observed what she conveyed to others only to destroy those features rather than heighten or control them as a model might.

"Ms. Harmon?"

"Yes?"

"I'm wondering if you can tell me a little bit about yourself."

"Well, I am originally from North Carolina. Have you heard of Duke?"

"Yes."

"I grew up outside of Durham. When we was little, my grandmother, God bless her soul, she used to take us to see the gardens beside the college. I have never seen anything so beautiful in all my life."

One of the most difficult things about having so little time to spend with people at Eastmark is that I can't talk to them at length about the experiences that give them pleasure. I have to assume that Ms. Harmon is here because something is wrong that she wants fixed. While I would prefer to hear the story of her life, to learn what strengthens her and what gives her faith and what sustains her, I have instead to direct my attention to what is most horrifying to her. The entire time I'm with her I have to try to answer the question: What is her problem?

"That's fine, Ms. Harmon, but you're at the emergency room of a mental hospital . . ."

"I know that."

"Good, good . . . and I need to find out what brings you here. To see if we can be of any help to you."

"Oh, all right."

Her face is a stiff mask. It expresses blankness. Or maybe it's not a mask at all, but what lies beneath the face she used to show to people. Perhaps this is as honest as it gets. She doesn't say a word. Now she pulls on her fingertips to amuse herself.

"Ms. Harmon, something happened, didn't it?"

"Mmm, hmm."

"What happened?"

"It happened when I went home." She sounds like she is

in a trance. "I went home for Easter to see my mother, and while I was there these men came by the house and they dragged me out, and then they took me into some woods where they raped me."

"Oh, no! That's awful!"

I still wonder why she came to a mental hospital for help. Her blankness suggests to me that her story is a metaphor, *in addition to,* or instead of, it being a true account. After all, Easter was two weeks ago. Could she have robbed her face of all its expressiveness in so short a time? Her blankness looks like the end result of a lifelong process rather than strictly the short-term effect of a recent violation. She may have been raped, but I wonder if before that her life contained the same sort of disasters. Are violation and abuse her story? Is blankness her idea of how she can best live with that tragedy? Perhaps she is in so much pain that her way to relieve it is to pretend that she is in no pain at all.

"My ex-husband, he was there. He was the ringleader."

"Are you OK? Did you go to the police? Have you been to a doctor?"

"I wanted to go to the police, but then he threatened me and told me that if I told anybody about what had happened that he would put up bail and get out and kill me. So I just kept my mouth shut. Until now."

"How do you feel right now?"

"That's not the worst of it."

"No?"

"That same evening he came back to the house for me, but this time I fought him off. While Mama slept, I fought him off in the kitchen until he got fed up with me and started whacking at my head with an axe."

"AN AXE??!"

"He just kept swinging away. He hit me nineteen times. I had over four hundred stitches."

"It's a wonder he didn't kill you," I say, and before I get to the end of my sentence I have a theory about all of this that I want to test. I put together in my mind Ms. Harmon's presen-

tation: her trancelike mien and behavior, her story with details
that do not make complete sense. I decide to take a chance.

"Ms. Harmon, did you run out of medicine?"

"Yes."

"What were you on?"

"Haldol."

This medication is used to moderate or extinguish some of
the symptoms of psychosis.

"Are you here to get a new prescription?"

"Mmm, hmm."

"What happened to your regular doctor?"

"Oh, him? He moved."

"Diagnosis?"

Fred is about to log Ms. Harmon into the notebook he uses
to record each of our cases. He has just done the follow-up
interview. She is in the waiting room.

"Schizophrenia, paranoid type, chronic," I answer dutifully.

"I agree," he says, and writes down the words next to her
name. He has a fine, old-fashioned script. "Disposition?"

"Antipsychotic medication and follow-up visits to the
clinic?"

"I'll give her a 'script' for some Haldol." Fred nods his
head. "That should straighten her out. And we'll have her come
back next Friday to see if it makes a difference, to see if she's
feeling any better."

I stand up and walk to the door. I am going to tell her our
decision. Fred stops me.

"Why don't you bring her back in for a moment? I'd like
to tell her myself. Because I think what's very important here is
her compliance with the medication. She's got to take the medicine or else she'll be right back here tonight out of her skull."

"Now, I don't want you fooling around," he says, with real
kindness, and with a sense of kinship to her suffering that surprises me, because his tone is brusque and authoritative, as al-

ways. "I know the medicine's not perfect. It makes your joints
stiff, and sometimes you get foggy, right?"

"How'd you know?" asks Ms. Harmon.

"Because I'm the doctor." He leans toward her on his elbows and she straightens up to move back. He stares at her and
says, "And I also know what happens when you don't take the
medicine."

"I gets crazy."

"That's right." He sits up. Fred is in control. He has made
a decision and accepted responsibility for it. "We want to put a
stop to that. I don't want to have to see you back here before
next Friday. Have this prescription filled and take the medicine
exactly the way I tell you to. OK?"

"OK, Dr. Kohl."

She walks out of the room. Fred turns to me.

"Good work," he says. "Who's next?"

Before we can deal with the next walk-in patient, a code
green is called in the Eastmark clinic foyer. James, Fred, and I
race out of the office. By the time we arrive, a bare-chested,
barefoot, young black man has been cornered by security and
male clinical staff and trainees. Flanagan, chief of security,
moves in. He tackles him. The man is quickly put in four-point
restraints. (His hands and legs are bolted to a gurney with tight-
ened pieces of cloth.)

Once when Jim was the D.O.C. (doctor on call, at night),
a man was brought in, face down, bolted to a stretcher. A sock
had been jammed into his mouth because the police were fed
up hearing him scream insults at them. It was two A.M. By the
time Jim took all the paperwork from the officers who had accompanied the man, and then moved to do a physical exam, this
patient, who had been left unattended, had suffocated and could
not be revived.

Death has not yet occurred during the day because unlike
the night when D.O.C.'s are on their own, the work is supervised.

■   ■   ■   ■

At the end of the day, I walk by the seclusion room in the locked unit. It's been unseasonably hot, but now things are cooling off. I see the patient who had been tackled by Flanagan. He is singing,

> "Get up! Stand up! Stand up for your rights!
> I say, get up! Stand up! Stand up for your rights!"

He dances in place. Soon he stops singing. Now he shouts the words. The sound can be heard from one end of the unit to the other. After a while, Betty Anne, the assistant head nurse, loses patience. She gets a doctor to give him a shot of Haldol so he can sleep. She can't work hearing his voice.

TERMINATION

TERMINATION
WITH STAFF

It is near the end of June. I find it hard to say good-bye. Will I be able to take enough from the experience? What *exactly* have I been given? Was it enough? Will I miss out when I leave? I don't know what I have taken in. Nor what I will remember. I want desperately to go, but then I hesitate. Although I know that it is impossible, that the internship is strictly for one year, I fantasize about sticking around. Maybe the best is still to come.

I create obstacles to avoid thinking about the end. I distract myself: I make lists. I ruminate about minor inconveniences (like wondering for days whether the gas company will correct their bill). I develop new projects and interests. I go shopping, and then in the store can't remember why I ever wanted the thing I'm about to buy. When all else fails, I pretend that there is no end. I'm just imagining it; it isn't really happening.

Woody Allen's joke about a vacation at a resort in the Catskills where "the food is terrible and there's never enough" exemplifies my thinking on endings. The internship may be a year in Hell, as one of my supervisors terms it, but why must it end so quickly?

I have had problems before with the endings of many important experiences. For example, after promising friends to see them at the last parties after graduation from Plainfield High School, I took off with Dawne, a girlfriend. After the Hampshire College commencement ceremony, I dodged friends again and chose to be with Fiona; we had met the day before. Following the final defense of my dissertation in clinical psychology at the University of Detroit graduate school, I drove straight to the airport. There is never closure. I didn't say good-bye to the teachers who still mean something to me, nor did I leave friends and acquaintances properly. I am aware of being sad about this, but the sadness is more like a thought rather than a feeling, and it doesn't bother me enough to change what has become a habit. Overwhelmed by my feelings, I try to turn them into thoughts.

But I am also the last one to know that a party, or a relationship, is over. I stand around waiting for an end when everyone else has already left. I try to convince a girlfriend that we can work things out even though she has made up her mind months ago to call it quits. My desire to preserve leads me to ignore the obvious: we have reached the end. Nothing can make the experience last longer. When I realize, finally, that it is time to go, I run away and devalue the loss.

Because I fail to accept the end, neither my feelings for others, nor what they mean to me, are conveyed adequately to them. I also prevent others from having an opportunity to tell me how I have figured in their lives. A sense of incompleteness dogs us. As a result, we go through life fragmented. Each new relationship is observed through a series of incomplete experiences. Everyone I meet, each new event, reminds me of the past.

It looks as though I am not the only one who has a problem with endings. Comm. Mental has virtually *institutionalized* the saying of good-byes into a formal process because the leadership does not want to leave it to chance. (Otherwise, we might all avoid it.) No intern or a resident ends the first year without participating in what Tom, super-chief of day hospital one, tells us, in hushed, reverential tones, to call:

THE TERMINATION PROCESS!

Beginning around the first of the year, which is only six months into training, we are asked by Tom to begin to devote time in meetings and in supervision to discussing how we feel about our termination in June. In April we are asked to start setting up individual, private appointments with all of the nurses and staff social workers with whom we have worked in order to discuss how we feel about termination with them. The closer we get to the end, the more time we spend talking about our feelings about the end. By the month of June, it is almost all we talk about in staff meetings, in team meetings, and in individual and group supervision.

"A good termination can be as important in therapy as everything that went on in the therapy up until that point," Edith, acting director of the psychology department, instructs us. "Saying good-bye stirs up all sorts of powerful feelings in us. We can't ignore them. We have to try and understand what they might be about. We have to talk about our feelings."

When I meet with other supervisors and staff to terminate with them, many of them talk about the termination process in their therapies, internships, and residencies. Robert tells me that the entire last year of his initial psychotherapy (prior to his psychoanalysis, which is now in its third year) was devoted to talking about what it will feel like to end therapy. Peggy says with a laugh that sounds more like a hiccup that she still can't end her therapy, now in its ninth year, because she dreads the idea of terminating with her therapist and that this dread is, ironically, what they talk about most in the therapy.

Alex Ellman does not talk about himself. Nor does he speak directly about the termination of his supervision of the work Carol and I have done with Mr. Plummer and Mr. d'Alvirs. He explains instead that we must be acutely sensitive to the feelings

of our patients when terminating with them because we are often
the most important person in their lives. Saying good-bye could
result in their decompensation (which means that when they
imagine and then see us abandon the relationship, their horror
and misery intensify and become intolerable for them). We move
on; often, as inpatients or as the chronic mentally ill, they simply change doctors. Each year or so, it is a new face for them, someone else to be interpreted or emotionally embraced by, someone
else whose loss they will have to mourn too soon.

The last meeting of the psychology department takes place, as
usual, in a small room that looks as if it used to be a walk-in
storage closet. Glassed-in cabinets on the wall facing us contain
stacks of old photocopied journal articles, kits to measure intelligence, and strange metal objects and equipment that look scientific but are equally useless. All of the interns are present:
Simone, Judith, Charlotte, Nick, Meg, and me. All of the staff
psychologists are here. The two secretaries have joined us all
year. Today is no exception.

The meetings have always been difficult to sit through because they begin with silence that may last as long as ten minutes. During this time, we all sort of look around the room or
at our closed appointment books—anything to avoid eye contact.
Then Edith or Peggy or Robert or Robin brings up a topic for
discussion. Like, how is everybody? And, how have referrals
for psychological testing been lately? Uh, is everything OK, you
guys? Hey, how come nobody's saying anything?

Because the department schedules this meeting immediately after the Saul Gold Group, on Thursdays, we come in a
little worn out. We're not so tired that we can't engage in conversation, but all of us are glad to cite that earlier group as the
excuse for our silence and discomfort here. It's certainly easier
to do that then to talk about what's really bothering us. That is,
until today, until this final meeting.

Judith, who is the bravest intern, the one who has always
been most willing to talk about her life openly, with complexity
and passion, says slowly, almost in a drawl, "I guess I feel

disappointed with the kind of relationship I've had all year with this department. Individually, I feel you're all great. But as a department that was supposed to protect and promote our needs in the hospital, I have to say that I feel you were a real failure.''

No one responds defensively. Silence is the first reaction. They listen to her and accept the judgment. It's almost as if they expected to hear it.

"I guess I feel sad,'' says Peggy. "I'm sorry that you feel like you were let down.''

I start to sweat and worry. Will it rain later on today? It looks like rain. Is my car door locked? There was a break-in in the hospital lot. Where am I going to live next week? My lease is up in the North End. How long will I stay with Laura in her apartment in Cambridge?

My anxiety guides me. It keeps me aloof from other feelings. Why am I so fearful?

I am afraid that if I speak up here, what I say will be invalidated via interpretation beyond recognition by the staff. For example, Robin excluded me from a study group (concerned with techniques of psychotherapy) that he formed outside the hospital near the beginning of the year. He felt that I was already overburdened by the demands of the internship. As a result, I expressed anger toward him. He listened politely, and then interrupted with: "Who are you *really* angry at?'' And when that only stunned me, since I was convinced that it was him I was angry at, *him!* Then he added, "It makes me sad to listen to your anger.'' Instead of challenging these remarks, I lost my place. I became confused and silent. After all, who knows how he would interpret and invalidate anything else I had to say? I thought I was angry at him, but by the time I left I was angry at myself! Ever since, I tend to let the other interns do the talking at these meetings. It feels safer that way.

"I feel it's too late,'' Judith continues, "too late for me to talk about being sad, Peggy. I'm through with being just sad. Because I'm angry, too. I want to know how this happened. I mean, you guys, you weren't available to us this year as a department that supported our needs.''

"I wish you had brought this up earlier," says Robin. "Because my sense is that you're right. As a department of psychologists, we allowed Prentiss Cliff and the psychiatrists to dictate to us. There wasn't enough of a dialogue between us and the psychiatrists."

"Why?" asks Simone.

"Historically," answers Edith, "it's always been that way. The psychiatrists see us as adjunctive to them. They don't want to share their power in the hospital."

"Well, why did you continue to allow that to happen?" Judith asks. "As a result of your *passivity,*" she spits the word out, "we ended up being trained largely by the psychiatrists. Which is fine, in a sense, because they were excellent as teachers and clinicians, but it's also a little strange, too, since, after all, we are going to become psychologists. And another thing: you're all behind the times, Edith. I mean, some of the psych. hospitals near my graduate school in California are run by psychologists! There's no reason why you couldn't have gotten more involved administratively at Comm. Mental if you'd had the energy or the inclination."

"I think," says Edith, and she bites her lower lip as tears well up, "I think I understand what you're saying."

"I hear you," says Peggy.

"It was a real drag." Now Judith is dabbing her eyes with a clotted tissue. "I know that the psychiatrists run this hospital. So? So what? Why wasn't the psychology department more involved with our internships on a day-to-day basis? Where were you guys when we had team meetings on the day hospitals? Or staff meetings? Or case conferences? Or at Eastmark? Except for supervision and this meeting, we hardly even saw you."

"Prentiss prefers things that way," says Peggy, repeating what's already been said.

"Why is that?"

"Because it's always been that way," Peggy repeats. "Boston is a very conservative and a very medical city. Psychiatrists run things here. They run the hospital."

"But that doesn't mean you have to go along with them!"

Uncharacteristically, Judith is close to shouting. "You can offer some resistance! Why be so passive about it? And if you want to go along with them, it certainly doesn't mean you have to involve us without explaining what we had in store! At the very least, you should have been up front about your relationship with the psychiatry department. It would have been a lot easier for us. Our expectations would have been very different."

"You're right," says Robin. "You're right, and I want to apologize. We should have been clear."

"That's OK," Judith says. She's crying a lot now. She's backing down, too. "That's fine. OK."

"It's not fine with me," says Charlotte. She's been silent at these meetings all year. Now that we have reached the end, she is strident, like a person who slams the door on the way out. "I wish we could have counted on you more."

Others join in. Nick whacks the table hard with his palms and says that he's furious. He's rarely just angry, always furious. Simone begins to cry a little.

"It's so sad and awful that it has to end like this," she says.

"Excuse me." Peggy leaps up, skips out of the room, and is sobbing.

"Great," says Judith, "just great. Now I've upset everyone."

All along Meg and I have said nothing. Perhaps this is what I've tried to avoid when I dodged endings before. Finally, however, I speak up, hesitantly, in a goofy, inarticulate whisper that is my idea of how people sound when they express feelings in this group, rather than a genuine expression of my sentiment. My talent for mimicry will be my downfall because one day, perhaps, I will forget the sound of my one true voice.

"I felt the same way as Judith did, all year, but I thought it was just me being nervous or something and so I didn't say anything, but it's not me, is it? I mean, we really have a problem here!"

"No, it's not you," says Robert, and he smiles patiently.

"Wow!"

Everyone laughs nervously, and for a few moments we can forget why we are so upset.

"I'm sorry I upset everyone," says Judith. She is drying her eyes. "Maybe it would have been better to maintain the pretense that everything is OK."

"I don't think so," Edith says as Peggy steps back in. She looks like she has taken a shower in her clothing. "I'm glad you said what you said. It had to be said. Maybe we can learn from it."

The room becomes silent again. I share in the other interns' outrage, but when I speak at these meetings I feel as if the staff looks at me like I am not making sense. I feel inhibited by them, as if I am behaving inappropriately and only they know it. I feel that they condescend toward me because I am not like them. They act strictly psychological. They interpret behavior while I prefer to try and observe it. I am not as interested as they are in seeing art as *sublimation,* or love as *object relations,* or religion as *metaphor,* or madness as *schizophrenia,* or misery as *depression.* I am not as interested as they are in definitions of human behavior or in limits to place upon it. I don't share their convictions in theories about why people behave as they feel they must. I feel that they miss an appreciation for the magical, for the invisible, for the accidental. As James Wells has said to me about his distaste for rigid, orthodox psychoanalysts, "There are things in heaven and in earth that they have not dreamed of."

But rather than confront these differences, I say as little as possible. As a result, not much is ever resolved between us.

Finally, Robin speaks up to try and end his discomfort: "I guess that's what your silences were about all year. There are some things that are very hard to say until it's time to go."

On the morning of my final day at Eastmark clinic, I suggest to James Wells and Zoe that we buy Fred Kohl a going-away present. I have something in mind. They agree at once.

The day is tinged with vague feelings of sadness, but no one talks about what comes next, or about the past year. We work harder than usual. The only other indication that this will

be our last Friday together comes after lunch when I tell Fred
that we have a gift for him.

"Well, let's see if we can knock off an hour early to celebrate," he says. "Who's the D.O.C. tonight?"

"Jeremy?"

"Ask Jeremy if he'll cover an hour early."

Jeremy agrees.

At 3:30 that afternoon, we huddle in Fred's office with a
brown paper shopping bag. James has taped a piece of paper
over the door's small window so that no one can see in.

"We wanted to thank you for a good year," I say. "So we
bought you a present."

Fred reaches in. He hoists up two tonic waters, four limes,
four plastic cups, and a quart of gin.

"Christ, that's nice of you all." Bifocals slip down his nose
as he lifts the bottle closer to examine it. Grinning broadly, he
winks and says, "Bombay, good stuff."

"It has been a pleasure to work with you, Fred," says
James.

"I really enjoyed it," Zoe says.

"Thanks a lot." I can't find more words to convey to him
my feelings about this departure. I'm overwhelmed by the im-
pending loss. I want to thank him for teaching me how to listen
to all sorts of people. He has a talent for being able to talk to
just about anyone: rich, poor, sober, drunk, miserable, elated,
stupid, genius, pompous, uncertain. He knows how to get people to talk about themselves. His respect for others' experiences
is more of a gift than a lesson. But all I manage to say is "I
learned a lot."

Fred says, "I know it's against the rules in this dump, but
how about sharing one drink with me?"

He uncorks the bottle. James slices the limes into quarters
with a penknife. I open a tonic water. Because its contents have
been contained under pressure and have been shaken up somehow, the liquid sprays out on us all. Zoe lines up the cups on
the desk. Fred pours gin. I pour tonic. James tops each cup with
a slice of lime.

"Cheers!" Fred says, looking us each in the eye steadily. "Cheers!"

The stuff is warm, but we drink it. For a while the four of us sit in the room, enjoying the merry spin that we begin to feel as the alcohol gradually kicks in. Soon we're chatting and laughing loudly about what we'll all be doing next year. Fred plans to stay put for a while, but he is going to cut back a bit. Zoe intends to spend her third and final residency year as director of an out-patient clinic attached to a hospital on Boston's north shore. James is looking for opportunities to teach the next group of first-year residents and for more out-patient work with higher-functioning patients. I am taking the summer off. In the fall I hope to get more involved with a Harvard Medical School research group, located at Cambridge City Hospital, that has asked me to join them in studying the psychological effects of the nuclear threat upon human behavior (the topic of my doctoral dissertation).

"Stay in touch, all of you," says Fred, as he corks the gin and packs up his gear lazily. "It's been a helluva year."

Carol and I meet in her office in order to terminate. It is primarily because of her (and Alex Ellman) that I understand the paramount importance of the family in this work.

"It was great working with you on the John Plummer case," she begins. "He's a difficult person to help, and because we both put a lot of effort into trying to understand him, the work was worthwhile. It wasn't easy at first. At all. But I think we both matured a lot over the year, and learned to work very well together. I'll miss that. And I feel that John will miss you, too."

"You've taught me a lot about families, Carol. Before I met you, I had no experience with family therapy. We weren't trained much along those lines in my graduate school. So you've really added to my appreciation of what has to be involved in helping someone."

"Thanks, Scott, it's nice to hear that. Sometimes I guess I feel that the social workers are taken for granted in the hospital. We don't get enough supervision, for example, and everyone knows where to find us when they want a favor, but when it comes time to involve us in a clinical decision, it's like we don't count at all.''

"It would be nice if we could help change that.''

"Yeah, because the way the hierarchy is set up at Comm. Mental, it's like the psychiatrists and psychologists use us to perform errands they don't want to do. I don't feel that our work is sufficiently valued.''

"You know I don't feel that way, right? Because I feel that I've learned as much from my work with you and Mr. Plummer as I have doing anything else in the hospital.''

"Thanks. I appreciate hearing that. I still can't imagine what it's going to be like working with your replacement. You really got John to trust you. It's not going to be easy to get him to trust the next doc just like that.''

"I'm going to miss him.''

"He was my favorite patient, too.''

"I guess I feel you've grown a lot.'' Tom puts out his cigarette abruptly. He looks embarrassed and preoccupied. "Initially, I felt you were preoccupied, you know, unable to complete the essential demands of the work, but over the year you learned how to pay attention to detail. You did good work with Plummer, Anastasi, and d'Alvirs, for example. All very difficult patients.''

"Thanks.''

"Uh, so, anyhow, anyway, how do you want to use this time? It's our last meeting of private supervision. Is there anything you feel that you need to tell me?''

"No, not really.''

We both say nothing. I try to sit still. Tom fidgets a bit. Our relationship over the year has been uneasy, but instructive. Tom has always been honest with me about my work, and I respect his abilities as a clinician, but we have never connected as people. We have kept distant from one another. For example, I don't know anything about his personal life, and he knows very little about mine. Terminating with Tom feels to me like closing a textbook. There is nobody to miss, only ideas, lessons, words.

"Well. Well, then. Well, then, why don't we use the time to talk a little bit about Mr. Anastasi. He's made a lot of progress, don't you think? And I like the treatment plan you've written up for him. It's gradual. It's structured. It's easy for him to understand. How did he react when you showed it to him?"

"Noncommittal."

"Yeah, I think that's to be expected. He's quite limited intellectually. But do you think he understood enough of it? Did you go over it in detail with him?"

"Uh huh."

"He understands the sequence? That he has to progress through various levels of supervised settings before we trust him to go out completely on his own?"

"Yes."

"OK. OK, then, I think we'll let him have a weekend pass in a few weeks."

"Do you think he'll be ready?"

"We'll see. I hope so. I'd like to see him on his way. He's been a lot of trouble. What do you think about his being ready?"

"I hope so, too. As long as he understands that there are consequences to his violence. And as long as we warn his ex-girlfriend that we're letting him out."

"Has that been taken care of, Scott?"

"He understands. And I've spoken to Jamie, who's the social worker involved, about getting in touch with his ex-girlfriend."

"OK, then. Well. Good year, Scott, good year."

The termination process on day hospital one culminates with a series of grand spectacles. Each psychology intern and psychiatry resident is required to speak before the entire assembly of staff at one of the final weekly meetings. The form of each presentation is the same. Jamie Armstrong, one of the senior staff social workers, is rumored to have organized and institutionalized the process. All the trainees must express aloud to every staff member in the room the feelings they have after working with that person all year. There are almost twenty people I must acknowledge publicly. My relationships with each one vary. This predicament is new to me. I've never had to leave a job before and say to each individual in the workplace what that person means to me. It is painful, weird, and unimaginable.

All of us put tremendous thought into how we're going to deal with this. John Kantrowitz asks Jamie if he can duck out, and she says, sure, go ahead, avoid your responsibility, ha-ha, but be prepared for staff to feel belittled and enraged. Never mind, he says. When it is time for him to say good-bye, he is businesslike, efficient, and considerate, as always. John is professional at everything he does: bloodless. In contrast, when her turn comes up, Katherine holds court. She flatters everyone. The praise is confectionery, but it's nice to be part of her illusion. She is *nice,* no more and no less.

Jim, Jeremy, Alice, and Judith give long talks, rich with genuine feeling and respect for the staff. Jeremy, who has become a great friend to me, makes people laugh by reciting a long, rhyming poem that weaves names and events together. His timing is perfect. As usual, he entertains splendidly. People cry listening to Judith describe the struggles she has shared with them. Jim encourages people to reflect upon and to consider how their life experiences impinge upon their work with the mentally ill. Alice's observations are simple and direct, unerring, and immensely kind.

It is difficult for each of us to perform like this. We are all very private about our lives. We enjoy being by ourselves. Through solitude, we remember the past. Our belief in the sensuality of memory helped direct our choice of the profession, and it has held us together as a group of trainees. To make a public statement about how we will remember staff who trained us to be clinicians is painful because it reveals what we usually keep hidden. Confession ought to be a private act. (But Jamie does not agree.)

When it is my turn to say good-bye, I have the usual jitters. Like Jeremy, I write down my talk, and this is some of what I say:

I believe that there is a Hindu parable about six
blind men and an elephant. Each man stands at a different part of the beast—tail, legs, torso, ears, tusk,
trunk—and describes the elephant from that perspective. It's only when they get together and compare notes
that their separate and equal perceptions allow them as
a group to understand what it is they are dealing with.

That's what working in the day hospital has felt
like this year. I have learned so much from everyone.
And if the idea of blindness suggests groping, I don't
mean that—blind people, in this parable, have a hands-
on experience. They don't observe from a distance.
The day hospital has been like that for me. It is a very
experiential place. I've learned to appreciate differences more than ever before.

It wasn't an easy year. The array of problems seen
in each individual patient often overwhelmed me. I
also still have plenty to learn about maintaining patients' charts and about setting limits on their disrup-
tive behavior. But it won't be a year that I will forget
at all, nor one about which I'll wonder: Did I learn
anything? And what I learned came so much from
working with everyone here. For that, I'm extremely
grateful.

Dolly, I learned three main things from you—
patience in work, courage in taking professional risks,
and enjoyment of the good lasagna you cooked for staff
parties.

Ellen, I loved doing the therapy group with you.
You have a wonderful sense of humor, an ability to roll
with the punches, and a feeling for life's goofiness that
was always a pleasure. You never lost your cool in the
group, and I appreciate that support.

Christina, I don't know what I can say to you
here. Your kindness and your skill at getting on others'
wavelengths are really quite unique.

Anton, you seem so calm and organized as a mental health assistant! You're always available to the patients, you never seem to panic or to be preoccupied. You always acted reasonably. Your work helped me to feel safer in the hospital.

Tom, I want to thank you for your patience and honesty. You always had something interesting to say about my work with patients. And I always felt like I knew where I stood with you with respect to the treatment I provided. We didn't always agree, but you were always direct and thoughtful. I admire your skill at diagnostics and your flexibility in letting people here work within pretty wide perimeters: we don't all have to do the same thing. That freedom to choose has been, I think, a better teaching point than how to maintain charts. Not that one should have to decide between the two! I also thank you for your constant availability when questions arose.

Jamie, this process of termination is your idea, right? Do you have any other ideas? High-wire balancing acts? Bear baiting? High-speed auto races? Anyhow, I like the way you speak articulately about patients here. I've had a wonderful time sharing cases with you, especially Eddie Anastasi.

Carol, I want to say that our work together with Mr. d'Alvirs and Mr. Plummer has been a great source of pleasure. Your interest and enthusiasm in family dynamics as a structure for understanding a patient's current and past predicament were really inspirational. You helped to change the way I feel about personality and how it develops.

Before the year ends, perhaps we'll have chances to say more to one another in other settings. Normally, I terminate with places by saying: See you later! And then I disappear. This termination process today—like so much else at Comm. Mental—has compelled me to experience the beast I have always avoided.

TERMINATION
WITH PATIENTS

The people who are the most difficult to leave are my patients. Despite the intimacy that has developed between us, we know that we won't see one another again when the internship ends, except in passing. Nor will I know about their lives anymore, except through rumors. Although the hospital administration has asked us to prepare in January for termination in June, the end of therapy is often ill-timed, an unnatural break in work that is just beginning. Many of these people lack contact with others in relationships of mutual love, respect, and trust, and the loss of a therapist can devastate them because without their therapist they are truly alone in the world.

When I consider their experience of solitude, the thoughts of D. W. Winnicott, the British psychoanalyst, come to mind. He speculates about the imaginings of the infant who is falling:

"going to pieces
falling for ever

dying and dying and dying
losing all vestige of hope of the renewal of contacts"

Most of my patients lack the means to prepare for the termination of their therapy. It will be a fundamental loss. After it ends, they will have to begin all over again, with the next crop of psychology interns and psychiatry residents. On July first, they will each be arbitrarily assigned a new trainee (unless they currently have as therapist a first-year psychiatry resident who elects to remain as doctor). And as if it is the most natural and logical step for them to take, they will have to begin talking about their pain, and their secrets, and their sorrow, with this complete stranger. If they are chronic and institutionalized, new shifts will occur for each of them, year after year, repetitively, for the rest of their lives. Eventually, with luck and persistence, they may develop a routine of sorts to gird themselves against the intrusive student of psychology who will ask on that first therapeutic meeting: What brings you here?

On the first day of June, I wake up from a dream about Mr. Plummer. I don't recall any of its details, only that I feel sad and frightened when I picture him this morning. He is an odd man of immense talent, like a king in exile from a land he can no longer remember. All he knows are rough details of grandeur, of the former expectations and victories that no one else sees any longer when looking at him: brilliant in high school, a student at Bowdoin College, the youngest child of two unsuccessful people who enshrined him as their one great hope for dignity. You need to read his history in the chart to find all that out! Because now and forever he has this strange disease he can't get rid of, that holds him in place like a man chained to a rock. Where is his kingdom? It has no location on the map. His connection to the future is effectively severed.

Now Mr. Plummer lives on the fringe, with bits and pieces of a life that do not make sense as a whole. For example, his intellect is prodigious, but he cannot readily assemble a statement that conveys a complete thought. The other patients on the locked unit look up to him, some even revere him, but he never talks to any of them. He speaks grandiosely of having magical powers, but needs a nurse to help him wash up.

We sit together in my office on the day hospital throughout the spring months. The sessions begin when I go to the locked unit and lead him downstairs. I push open my door. Then we walk in together. He takes a seat. I sit facing him. My desk is flush to the wall so that there are no solid barriers between us.

The room is furnished sparsely: an old wooden desk, some old chairs, a dirty throw rug, a few art prints of French impressionist landscapes, and a standing lamp that has between its base and top a Formica tray stained dark brown so as to resemble wood. Above the desk I've tacked up a poster depicting Egyptian hieroglyphs. Its symbolic language reminds me of the way in which patients communicate here.

For example, when I ask Mr. Plummer how he feels he says, "There's snow on the roof but none in the basement." "Snow," "roof," and "basement" don't mean the same to him as they do to me. He uses a single word to signify his complicated inner states, feelings, thoughts, memories, visions—but who knows? Perhaps the function of words differs for him. The dissimilitude of meanings in language between us makes the development of a relationship feel close to impossible some of the time.

The language of patients here is also like hieroglyphs because in it are signs that cannot be deciphered easily, and that are suggestive of ancient periods in their lives. But there is no certain way like the Rosetta stone that led the way to the deciphering of the Egyptian hieroglyphs to guide my interpretation of the meanings each patient conveys to me through his symbolic language. The codes or signs used in schizophrenic language vary from person to person because one schizophrenic is like no other schizophrenic, just as one neurotic is like no other neurotic. The diagnosis describes only facets of a huge life. The great mistake is to assume that it describes everything about a human being, rather than a narrow set of expectations and observations, because each schizophrenic requires a different sort of treatment and a unique relationship with the therapist, rather than identical medication and psychotherapy.

When I have tried to talk with Mr. Plummer about termination, he has refused to be direct. He prefers to say nothing. When he talks, his monologues are about his powers of mind-reading, telekinesis, visions of the future, all things magical. I recognize that he uses signs to explain his feelings and thoughts about termination, but his unwillingness to be more direct is driving me crazy.

At the same time, his psychosis is intermittent. For example, he makes perfect sense when he talks angrily about a medication's unpleasant side effects, while at other points in the same conversation, I have no idea what he is trying to say.

And then there are the times when he is mute. That's when we sit together and both say nothing. It's hard for me to sit in a room with someone and say absolutely nothing. I tend to explain myself through words, not through gesture. Maybe I have less-complicated matters to try and explain.

By June, I begin to devalue the importance of Mr. Plummer's psychotic remarks and silence in our sessions. He may want to terminate the therapy through wordlessness and through madness, but I feel the need to end with language that expresses meaning to us both. I can also picture my supervisors in the room, egging me on to do this, insisting, saying, "GO ON! ASK MR. PLUMMER HOW HE FEELS! DON'T BE AFRAID TO CONFRONT! DON'T BE SO VAGUE!" He won't respond sensibly to my questions, but I get compulsive about trying to please the imaginary supervisors.

Weeks go by fruitlessly until there's only one session left.

"How are you feeling, John?"

"The medicine you give me is poison." He does not move. His posture suggests to me a wooden Indian. "I do not want to take it any longer."

Since we've both heard him say this a hundred times before I think a while about what else he may be trying to tell me now.

What does it have to do with termination? He must be bringing it up today as a way of talking about his feelings about termination. I take a guess at his meaning. I know he hates the medicine. Maybe that feeling is what he is trying to convey. Maybe he also hates the idea of me leaving.

"I wonder if you feel sad and angry because I'm leaving, and all that it seems like I'm leaving you as I depart is medicine."

"The poison makes me feel like a mummy," he says as an answer to my observation.

I'm still thinking that he's trying to talk about termination using the topic of medication as a metaphor for his feelings. Why would he tell me that he feels like a mummy? He's never used that phrase before to describe his hatred of medication. Does it have to do with something in my office? I think of my poster of the hieroglyphs. That's pretty magical-looking stuff, right up his alley. Suddenly I wonder if there is a connection:

"Mummies are dead kings, right?"

"Dead *pharoahs*," he corrects me.

He looks interested in what I'm saying. I mean, after all, he's still talking to me. He hasn't started one of his monologues where I get lost, and he's not mute yet. So maybe I'm on the right track. Why does he feel like a mummy? How does a mummy feel? I guess again:

"I think what you're saying is that the medication makes you feel robbed of your powers."

"Yes," he says, smiling back at me. He rarely smiles. It feels as if he has given me a gift.

And then he says, with so much clarity that I am startled, as if wakened from a deep sleep by the sound of a crashing window in my apartment—someone is breaking in!—"It's hard when a reliable therapist leaves. We've grown to trust each other, and your leaving is like cutting a flower before it's had a chance to blossom."

I don't know what to say. He has spoken with so much sadness, and all at once. I never expected to hear this from him. Now I'm the one who's mute.

After some time passes, I feel I have to respond with equal emotion—although this is certain to be difficult because I have been distant at times as a way of preserving my sanity. When I am expressive with him, I am afraid that I will be swept away by his madness.

Taking a deep breath, I say, "I'm going to miss you, too, John. I'm sorry that we have to stop working together."

"If you really wanted to stay you could, you know."

"Well, no. I can't. I can't, really, because . . . because the internship ends, and . . . and I have to move on."

"I said, *if you really wanted to stay.*"

"No I couldn't, really, even if I wanted to, because I'm a psychology intern, you know that, John, and after one year our training year is over."

Why am I suddenly unable to respond to his feelings about termination? He's trying to tell me that he's angry about my leaving, and I'm talking to him about the practicalities of staying on. I guess his anger frightens me. I guess I feel guilty about the pleasure I feel in ending the work.

"You could if you wanted," he insists again. "You could arrange it with the administration."

"I suppose," I concede, "I suppose that's true."

"OK, then." He smiles. He takes a parting shot: "It's important for us to be honest with one another."

I smile, too, at his having turned the tables on me by lecturing like a therapist to a patient about how therapy has to work.

And then we sit and say nothing. Like a minute of silence to honor the dead. It is a familiar place for us both by now, and when I glance at the electric clock on my desk to see how much time is left in the session, Mr. Plummer stands up abruptly and says, "I would like to go upstairs."

"We still have a few minutes left."

He doesn't answer me. He stands up, walks to the door, and fumbles with its knob. I take him back to the locked unit.

When I return to my office, I cry, missing him.

■   ■   ■   ■

On the last day, I imagine hearing a bell ring. It must be three o'clock in the afternoon on the last day of school. Mrs. Jefferson, my fourth-grade teacher, says: "Have a nice summer! See you in September!"

I can't wait to unfold my hands and get up from my wooden chair in the third row of the classroom.

It will be wonderful to have nothing to orient me. The internship has been all-encompassing, completely overwhelming, an experience that I imagine is like being in the military. I think about Comm. Mental all the time, but I never talk about what goes on there when I am away because I am sick of the place.

Without the hospital, I will be lost, which will be terrific, of course, for a change: no appointment books, no responsibilities, no meetings, no supervisors. I will be free again to read novels, or to sleep late, and do absolutely nothing.

Judith, John, and I drive to Charleton's, a bar in Brookline, to celebrate the end. Although John is starting his second year in psychiatry on July first, he wants to say good-bye to us with a few beers. We drink, and tell jokes about our colleagues, and there's a breathless quality to our conversation, as if we have just completed a mission of great secrecy and importance, and are now free, finally, to be ourselves.

At the hospital, we were reined in. Working with the mentally ill does that. It is difficult to show feelings around institutionalized (or semi-institutionalized) people whose emotions are often strange or guarded—it's like having a meal in front of someone who's hungry and not offering anything to that person to eat.

John returns home to his wife. Judith is going to meet a friend. I drive to Cambridge. Before I see Laura, I stop in Harvard Square to buy books to read over the next few weeks: Henry Miller's *Tropic of Cancer* and *Tropic of Capricorn*. In typical fashion, I *plan* to be spontaneous. I *plan* to be physical rather than cerebral. I *plan* to have a good time this summer. I am getting sick of planning all the time! Maybe that means it's time to stop planning!

Jeremy and his wife Janice meet us for dinner. Like John,

Jeremy is also entering his second year of the psychiatry residency, but because we have become close over the year, we have decided to celebrate the end of my internship together.

We eat at Frank's Steak House in North Cambridge. Frank's is a restaurant in a working-class neighborhood where people celebrate birthdays, first dates, anniversaries, retirements. We drink, laugh, tell stories. It's like we've won the war.

When we return to her apartment, I ask Laura to mark the end of the internship by piercing my ear, which she does—pop!—painlessly with an ear piercer she has taken from her office for the occasion. It's like getting a tattoo.

And that's how I think things come to a close. But it isn't quite over yet.

Three weeks later, when I am at Comm. Mental for the weekly meeting of the Saul Gold group, I run into Jim.

"I'm sorry, Scott," he says somberly. He puts a hand on my shoulder, purses his lips and looks at his feet. "I'm really sorry."

"Sorry about what?"

"Don't you know?"

"Know what?"

"Wow. No one called you?"

"Jim, what happened?"

"Anastasi killed himself over the weekend."

"Omigod."

"I can't believe you didn't know, that no one told you."

"How'd it happen? What happened?"

"I was the D.O.C. Maybe I should have called you."

"Jim, what happened?"

"Well, for the first time in years he went home to his apartment. On a twenty-four-hour pass. When he didn't show up the next morning, we sent the police by to check on him. They found a suicide note. He jumped off the Tobin Bridge. He killed himself. In the evening, they recovered the body."

"Oh, God."

"Yeah. Yeah."

"What did the note say?"

"Jamie said that it said something like, 'I'm tired of being a pain in the ass to everybody.' "

"Wow. So all along we were treating him like he was a threat to others when he was really a threat to himself."

"Or both, or both."

"How does his new doc feel about it?"

"Well, he's devastated. I mean, imagine starting your psych residency and three weeks later having a suicide. It's like your worst nightmare of what could happen happening. He feels awful. You should talk to him."

"Jesus."

"Yeah."

"Well," I say—and now I can feel myself starting to make excuses, and trying to distance myself from this tragedy—"Well, I don't really feel like it's got a whole lot to do with me, you know, because I terminated with him three weeks ago. He was no longer my patient."

"I don't think it's your fault," says Jim. "But you must have feelings about losing him."

"No, I do, I do. But it's not the same as losing a patient when he's my patient because he hasn't been my patient in a while. I mean, I terminated with him three weeks ago."

"I know."

"And so I feel badly, of course, but it's not the same as feeling responsible."

"I don't think you are responsible. I don't think anyone's responsible! If someone wants to die, they'll find a way to do it."

"Right, right," I say, still keen on being absolved by Jim. "But he wasn't my patient, is what I'm trying to say. I didn't make the decision to have him go on that twenty-four-hour pass. Whoever made that decision must feel responsible."

"Scott, you can feel responsible without being responsible. Look, it's easy for me to say that, he wasn't my patient. I know how you must feel."

"He wasn't my patient either, Jim. I terminated with him three weeks ago."

I telephone Tom. He says, "It's sad news, but he was a very sick man, Scott, and I think he was determined to put an end to his life. I have to admit that I'm surprised because I never thought of him as depressed."

"I didn't either. Who did?"

"No one. I mean, we all thought of him as an antisocial personality disorder with a seizure disorder and atypical psychosis, or maybe a schizoaffective disorder, I don't know, and we were all afraid of him, and now look."

"How's his family feel about it?"

"Frankly, I think that they're glad in some ways to see an end to it all. He's been a source of profound stress for them. I think he knew it, too. He felt like a burden to them. By killing himself it's like he's taken off the weight he imposed on them."

"It's so strange, because the entire time he was here, he kept insisting that nothing was wrong with him. That if we would just let him go home, everything would be fine."

"He must have misjudged the situation," says Tom. "It was a fantasy. Because when he went home he must have realized that he was more comfortable, and more at home, locked up here in the hospital. That must have really scared him. He couldn't allow himself to admit that. Because what kind of admission would that have been? How could he have adjusted to the fact that he is mentally ill and chronic? What kind of life is *that?*"

In a week, on Sunday, Laura and I are walking in the Public Garden, which is below the Boston Common. It is late July, and the tourists are out, as well as many beds of flowers. As we head up a small rise, toward a footbridge that will take us over a pond in which the swan boats are crossing, I see Mr. Plummer walking along, about thirty feet away, out on a day pass. He is wearing pajamas, over which he has on a gold brocaded vest. He has on green foam hospital slippers. On his head is a towel

shaped to resemble a turban. With his goatee and one looped
gold earring, he looks like a fortune-teller. His eyes are wide
open, but unfocused, as if he is seeing events unfold around him
from a great distance across the universe.

Laura sees him, too, and never having met the man before,
never having heard me talk about him, she says, "Look at that
guy! Isn't he weird-looking? You're the psychologist. What do
you think is wrong with him?"